D1230122

C.1

917.4745 Lape
Lape, Fred.
A farm and village boyhood.

DATE DUE		
JUL 09 1996		
JUL 2 6 2000		
MAR 2 1 2001		
MAR 1 7 2005		
APR 0 9 2005		
JUN 0 9 2007		

OCT 3 1 1980

VESTAL PUBLIC LIBRARY

0 00 10 0091532 0

VESTAL PUBLIC LIBRARY
VESTAL, NEW YORK 13850

A Farm and Village Boyhood

A York State Book

A Farm and Village Boyhood

FRED LAPE

Foreword by
LOUIS C. JONES

SYRACUSE UNIVERSITY PRESS
1980

Copyright © 1980 by SYRACUSE UNIVERSITY PRESS
Syracuse, New York 13210

All Rights Reserved

First Edition

This book is published with the assistance of a grant
from the John Ben Snow Foundation.

Part of Chapter 2 first appeared in *The Humanist*, November/December 1972,
and is reprinted by permission.

Library of Congress Cataloging in Publication Data

Lape, Fred, 1900–
A Farm and Village Boyhood.

(A York State Book)
1. Lape, Fred, 1900– 2. Esperance, N.Y. —
Social life and customs. 3. Esperance, N.Y. —
Biography. I. Title
F129.E88L364   974.7'45 [B]   80-17303
ISBN 0-8156-0162-X

Manufactured in the United States of America

Contents

Fred Lape, a teacher, poet, writer, and farmer, is director of the George Landis Arboretum in Esperance, New York, and is the author of *Apples and Man* and several volumes of poetry.

Foreword

This book is the autobiography of the author down to his
eighteenth year, but more especially it is concerned with the
structure and personalities of a small turnpike village, Esperance, New York, and its surrounding farm folk — character
profiles Fred Lape draws with humor, earthiness, and economy
but without any nostalgic patina.

The importance of the work lies in the remarkably
detailed and intimate picture of domestic life just above the
rural subsistence level. It is a bonanza for the student of social
history, folk life, or domestic economy: the foods and how they
were cooked, his debunking of the myth of "good old country
cooking," ways of the farm and barnyard, the tensions in rural
households, the balance of the hard, ill-paying labor and the
beauties of nature in Upstate New York.

On another level it diagnoses the erosion of a turnpike
village that prospered in the last half of the nineteenth century,
not only as a service area for surrounding farms, but for the
heavy traffic on the Cherry Valley Turnpike, Route 20. Then
came the railroad, missing the village, and the great industrial
development of the Mohawk Valley to the north. Esperance
had become an intellectual center of sorts, and all that passed

before 1900. So it is a village in decline, drained of its best brains, its businesses wilting before a more vigorous technology, its mind closing, unresponsive.

This is the story — seldom told — of hundreds of New York State villages, and one well told here. It is a pleasure to read, bringing back to me (a half dozen years the author's junior) sights and smells, events and embarrassments long forgotten.

Cooperstown, New York   Louis C. Jones
Summer 1980   *Director Emeritus*
              New York State Historical Association

Oak Nose Farm

My first summer on a farm was spent in a one-room slab shack in an orchard. It was 1902. I was two years old. My father built the shack out of hemlock two-by-fours and slabs sawed from the farm woodlot. It was ten by twelve and about seven feet high at the eaves. It contained a bed, a cook stove, a handmade table, two chairs, and a few shelves for dishes. There was a door, there were two windows, there was a carpet on the floor. When my mother swept, she opened the door and sent the dust flying out over the grass. We started to live in it in May, when the apple trees were just shedding their petals, and dandelions and buttercups were blossoming among the orchard grasses.

I have three distinct memories of the summer. I remember the yellow hemlock boards of the ceiling, which I must have stared at many hours from the bed. I remember a gray flannel dress that I wore. At that time all children of two or three, boys and girls alike, wore knee-length dresses. And I remember being stung by a bee and being put into a wooden washtub, either to cool me off and remove the sting, or perhaps to stop me from squalling, for I was a squalling brat.

The farm was not my father's. It was known as the

The slab shack, 1978.

Silvernail farm. There was a good colonial farmhouse, built about 1860 by Coonrad Silvernail. Now my grandfather was running the farm, by virtue of his having married for his second wife Mahala, the third of the Silvernail sisters. There were two other Silvernail girls still living, Maria and Jane, spinsters in their sixties. There would have been room in the Silvernail house for us too, but my father was always an independent man, and even for a summer preferred the slab shack in the orchard. It is also probable that knowing the Silvernail vagaries and my mother's temperament, he considered the slab shack safer.

It was, I believe, one of the happiest summers my father and mother ever spent. It had all the novelty of a new way of living. It left the two of them to themselves, and they still liked each other's company. Night after night my father said, "This is the way to live."

The view from the shack was only of apple trees and grass and sky, but the view from the Silvernail stoop, as all porches thereabouts were then called, was beautiful. It was a well of space with the Schoharie Crick — the maps call it a creek, but it was never so pronounced — lost at the bottom behind the tops of descending woodlots. The Schoharie, on its sometimes tempestuous course from the Catskill Mountains north to the Mohawk River, wriggled a right-hand turn from east to north at the village of Esperance, at the upper tip of Schoharie County. The Silvernail farm was on the inside of this turn, and the opposite valley wall was like a wide glacial cirque which had become fertile and farmed and checkered with fencerows and woodlots and meadows. All of this lay just beyond the Silvernail yard and the dirt road that edged it. But as on many other New York and New England farms, the indifferent Coonrad Silvernail had built a pigpen between the house and the road, so that from the stoop one looked directly upon the hog run, and on east wind days got the smell of it in the nose.

My father helped that summer with the farm work. He was himself just in the making-up-his-mind stage of becoming a farmer. In his teens he had been apprenticed to the watch repairer's trade and for several years had run a jewelry shop in Holland Patent, New York. But the early death of my sister had poisoned his living there. Since coming back to Esperance he had taught school for two winters. But he had grown up on a farm, and the farm was beginning to call him back. Already he was saying to my mother, "A farmer's life is the only independent life."

Emma Happe Lape and Herman F. Lape, the author's

parents, c. 1890, the time of their marriage.

The orchard around the house was part of our living. In June the grass was full of ripe strawberries. Where the red devil's paint-brush spread among timothy and clover, there the strawberries clustered close to the ground. My mother would go out before breakfast and pick enough for the three of us. Often at night she would make strawberry shortcake. The base was slightly sweetened baking powder biscuits that came out of the cookstove oven with their tops browned like meerschaum pipes, and opened to a white froth of biscuit, down which the red berry juice trickled.

After the strawberries came raspberries. These grew in thickets along the fences, and my mother never liked to pick them because there was always danger of meeting a snake. The snakes were all harmless and slithered away from my mother as fast as she ran from them, but she feared them with an unreasoning fear as if they were rattlers. Sometimes there would be a bush or two of blackcaps, but these were so delicious raw that we always ate the sweet purple berries with the white bloom as fast as we picked them.

In July the harvest apples began to ripen. First came the Yellow Transparents, and then soon the Red Astrachans, which make the best of all apple jellies. About this time too the Sweet Bough tree in front of the Silvernail house began to ripen its fruit. My father working in the haying would grab an apple from the tree when he went past with the empty hay rigging on the way to the field for a load of hay, and munch it as he went, holding the lines in one hand and the apple in the other.

When the hay had been moved from most of the meadows, my mother and I went for blackberries. I always got scratched, and I squalled. Oat harvest was beginning now, and the first wild apples were ripening on the trees along the stone walls. We never used them, for the orchard was full of better ones, but we never passed a tree without sampling its fruit, often so sour that it puckered the face. Yet the tangy juice of many of them was pleasant.

Last of the season's berries were the elderberries, slowest to ripen and strongest in flavor. They grew in wet places, hanging their heavy black clusters of small fruit over the fences or brooks. My mother canned them for winter pies.

And now with fall the orchard around the house was as beautiful as it had been in May. All the trees hung loaded with fruit, Greenings with brownish cheeks, Northern Spies streaked with red and yellow and green, long pointed Sheep's Noses with somber green and dark red streaks, and tight little Russets, whose yellow green skin was like brook water flecked with sunlight and the bottom shadow of brown leaves. The smell of them was in the air, as sweet as the smell of flowers. Later, in barrels, they would perfume the cellar of the Silvernail house.

That summer my father made up his mind. He went back down to the village of Esperance that winter to teach school, but it was for the last time. In midwinter he bought the farm above the Silvernail farm, and in spring we moved to it.

The farm cost twenty-five hundred dollars. My father had saved fifteen hundred toward it. For the remaining thousand he took out a mortgage, which was to dog him for half of the rest of his life. The interest on the mortgage at 6 percent amounted to sixty dollars a year. It sounds picayune now, but yearly it was a shadow that hung over the household. For two months before it was due there was saving and scrimping, and sometimes the fear that there would not be enough money to pay it.

The farm that my father bought lay next to the Silvernail farm. Its views were more dramatic, and it was for this more than for its fertility of soil that my father bought it. He loved steep slopes and far views.

The buildings stood on a knoll at the foot of a semicircle of hills. The barn, near the edge of the knoll, commanded the better view of the valley. The house stood more in the shelter of the hills, close to the road. It was a typical L-shaped New York farmhouse, built about 1840, of hemlock taken from the farm woodlot. The beams were hand hewn, the downstairs floors of six-inch joined hemlock, the upstairs floors of eighteen-inch white pine. The front hall had a cherry railing and newel post. The ceilings of the upstairs rooms slanted down under the roof at the sides of the house to small three-paned windows. One distinctive feature of the house was that the door and window frames of the main wing slanted in toward the top like Egyptian temple doors. I have seen the same feature in a few other houses of the period, but only in this area. It may have been the original idea of some local carpenter.

There were no conveniences, neither electricity nor water toilet. There was a water line running from a well behind the house to the cellar, but the water had a sulphurous taste that made it unpleasant for drinking, and it was too hard to be good for washing. The water from the drinking well in the front yard was excellent. The privy was at the end of an open woodshed that completed the wing of the house. It was more protected and warmer in winter than many I have used. (The worst I have ever known was behind a farmhouse at Bailey's Island, Maine. It was built on a steep slope, backed to the sea, and in a good wind the updraft was so strong that the toilet paper would never go down, but always leaped from the hand and floated in the air like a dried leaf.)

It was from the high meadows that one saw the real beauty of the farm. One section sloped to the north, looking down through the open V of the Schoharie and across the Mohawk River to the Adirondack Mountains, whose blue

The ancient white oak after which the farm was named.

ridges on clear days fluted the horizon. Another knoll of pasture, jutting out from the woodlot, was crowned by a single white oak some six feet in diameter at the base. Under this tree, whose trunk was marked by two wriggling lightning scars, one could see in the near valley the clustered houses of five villages, Esperance, Quaker Street, Braman's Corners, Eaton's Corners, and Burtonsville, and in the distance the peaks of the Catskills in the south and the Adirondacks in the north. On quiet or east wind days one could hear the rumble of horses and wagons going over the wooden bridges at Esperance and at Burtonsville. This was of all places on the farm the spot my father loved. It was the spot to which he always took visitors, and from the promontory of land upon which the oak stood he gave the farm its name, Oak Nose Farm.

The land itself was varied. The flats were drained swamps of deep black soil, fertile but difficult to work, particularly in wet seasons. The hillsides were rocky and lean. The earth ribs of sandstone and shale stuck out on the pasture slopes. Some layers of the sandstone were hard and easily quarried. Two small quarries on the farm had furnished the foundation and cellar walls of the house. Scattered indiscriminately over the flats and slopes lay either buried or on the surface the quartz and granite boulders that the glaciers had left on their last withdrawal.

This was Oak Nose Farm, rich in some ways, but basically lean for farming. It was pleasant in summer, beautiful but cold in winter. Sometimes the thermometer dropped to twenty below with a gale howling. Sometimes the roads were drifted full with banks of snow ten feet deep, and the only way to town was go to around through the fields. All the roads were still dirt. In the spring they were sometimes axle deep in mud, and on the flats there were sink holes into which a buggy might plunge up to its wheel hubs and be stuck. Even late in May when the surface of the road had dried, these sink holes lingered, caked and dusty over the top but still unsure to the foot.

To avoid the spring mud my father moved in March with a sleigh. March is usually a winter month in the Schoharie Valley. The worst snows often come then, and frequently zero degree days. When the snow goes, the lingering snowbanks are covered with dust from the fall plowed fields. The hills and meadows are dingy and brown, the sunless March days gloomy and forbidding.

To my mother, who had never lived on a farm before except for the previous summer in the slab shack, and who knew nothing about the real work of a farmer's wife, it was a harsh shock. The cold, damp, unsettled house was depressing, the dirty landscape forbidding. Furthermore, my grandfather and stepgrandmother were to come up from the Silvernail farm and live with us. Now my mother and the notions of the Silvernails, embodied in Mahala, were to be cooped up in one house. So the seeds of discontent were sown.

But my father was oblivious to all this. He was full of enthusiasm that he at last had a farm of his own. And my grandfather was for a time to be the keeper of peace. He was a gentle man. He brought his stock with him, and when he walked up the road his pigs followed behind him like children.

So my mother became a farmer's wife. All farmers' wives of those days worked hard. They kept their houses clean or left them dirty, according to their makeup. But always they had to cook and wash dishes, to bake bread and pies and cakes, to make butter, to can vegetables and fruits and meats in season, to sew, and in the haying time to help the men in the fields. In the kitchen they expected no help from the men, and got none. They were up in the morning as soon as, or before, their men folk. They prepared breakfast while the men were in the barn doing chores.

Cooking was always done on a woodburning stove, but in order to avoid its heat in summer, an extra cookstove was usually put in the woodshed or in some outer and better ventilated room called the summer kitchen.

Much has been written about farm cooking, most of it romantic slush. At its best it was excellent, at its worst terrible, at the average slightly below mediocre. The cake which the farmer's wife took to a church social was apt to be luscious, but the daily cake on her own supper table could be tasteless and stale. The specials were good, fricasseed chicken with biscuits and gravy, creamed young potatoes and peas, suet pudding. But many of the ordinary foods were poorly cooked. Not many farm women cooked their meats tastefully. They usually overcooked them, and whatever meat was put into the pot or oven, whether pork, beef, lamb, or veal tasted about the same when it was put on the table. Vegetables were usually overcooked, except the few like carrots and beets and turnips which are best after long, slow cooking. Their mashed potatoes, when prepared for a company meal, were creamy and delectable, but their daily boiled potatoes were soggy and unappetizing.

Breakfasts were heavy, oatmeal, ham or bacon and eggs, and fried potatoes. But the unique breakfast of the region was buckwheat pancakes. Many women baked them daily for breakfast all year around. The batter was kept in an earthenware pancake pitcher in the cellarway.

Since the old-fashioned raised buckwheat pancake is a nearly forgotten food, but a delicious one, I give here the recipe. To start the batter mix in the evening pure buckwheat flour with buttermilk or sour milk to form a batter the consistency of a thin cake batter. Add salt to taste and a small amount of yeast. Let this stand in the pancake pitcher overnight in a warm room. In the morning, just before using, dissolve a level teaspoon of baking soda in a small amount of hot water, pour into the batter, stir rapidly, and start baking the cakes at once. They sound simple. Actually they are difficult to make without experience. One must learn two things, just how much soda to add and how to bake the cakes. Too much soda tastes bitter in the cakes, too little leaves the cakes soggy and sour. The baking of a buckwheat pancake is more difficult than the baking of a wheat pancake. The griddle must be hot and the cake must be turned very quickly, the moment it has crusted over on its under side. If the cake is let bake too long without turning, it will lose all its air, and when done will look and taste like a piece of dried teboard. But a buckwheat cake well baked is a warm rich brown overlaid with a fine network of black lines like a lace mantilla.

Whatever batter is left over from the meal is left in the pancake pitcher and set in a cool place. Pancake pitchers were of earthenware, and a handmade wooden paddle was used to stir the batter. Our pitcher was a highly glazed dark molasses brown Bennington one with a hunting scene embossed around the sides. Each night a new amount of flour and buttermilk and salt were added, but no more yeast. The remaining batter furnished a continually replenished yeast supply.

We always ate our buckwheat pancakes straight from the griddle, while their surfaces were still crisp, before the cakes had time to steam through. To assure this my mother usually baked while the rest of us ate, managing now and then to slip a cake on her own plate and take a bite of it while she was running back and forth from the stove to the table. A pancake was usually garnished with butter and maple syrup.

I used to like buckwheat pancakes even cold. Sometimes my mother would fix the left-over ones for my school lunch, buttering them and rolling them up with jelly into a cylinder, as Mexicans eat tortillas.

When the breakfast dishes were washed, the customary job during my childhood was churning. Churning was almost a daily task during the summer months. When I was quite young, the only churn was the old barrel type, with a wooden splasher that worked up and down through a hole in the cover. At that time either my grandfather or my father had to do the churning. But soon the cradle churn came in, and this I was able to operate as soon as I was seven or eight years old.

I hated churning. Anyone who has churned one churnful of reluctant cream can easily understand why earlier and more superstitious generations believed that witches often put spells on cream, for if the temperature happened to be not right or the cream not quite sour enough, that dull unchanging slop of the cream that went on inside the churn minute after minute for half an hour, three-quarters of an hour, an hour, an hour and a half, could exasperate the sweetest temper.

Once the butter had come, my mother's job was to work the butter, salt it, let it stand, work it again, and pack it into butter crocks. The butter was sold either to regular customers in the village or to the grocery stores. We usually packed away some crocks of butter made during the clover season for next winter's use, for grass butter is sweeter than winter hay butter. It was covered deeply with a layer of salt over a piece of cloth, tied up with cloth and paper, and stored in the cellar.

Along with the churning and butter making, whatever baking of pies, cakes, and bread was necessary, and preparations for the noon dinner, which was the big meal of the day, would be going on. After the dinner dishes were washed and put away, my mother had, if any time, her slack hours. But of course there was always a basket of clothes to be mended, socks to be darned, lamps to be filled, stoves to be blacked.

Supper, usually held about five o'clock, was more or less of a pickup meal. Perhaps the leftovers from dinner were warmed up. Bread and milk was a common supper dish everywhere in the community, with cheese or raw onions or dried herring for side flavoring. And in our family there were the ever-present pies and cakes. My father thought that a meal without pie or cake, or better both, was not a meal at all. However, he did not insist on either being fresh, so in general my mother baked several pies and a large cake once a week. She was also apt to carry this same work-saving method with other foods, particularly with baked beans. I still can hear my father say, in a slightly aggrieved tone, when we had sat down to the same dish of baked beans for the fifth meal, "Emma, do you *have* to make so many beans at one time?"

When the supper dishes were washed and put away, there was time for my mother to sit down by the kerosene lamp on the kitchen table and read the daily paper or darn socks or more likely fall asleep in her chair for weariness.

In the haying season she helped in the field, drove the team for the horsefork at the barn, drove the team for the dump rake, and sometimes loaded hay, jobs that I was later to take over when there was more housework because of a hired man. And in season she picked berries in the fields, canned fruit and vegetables, and helped in the butchering and curing and canning of the meats.

It was a hard life. Compared to the average household work of today, it seems unbelievable. Yet many farm women of the time did it cheerfully and remained healthy doing it. They had little time to be lonely. They exercised too much to become neurotics. Usually, as the tombstones testify, they outlived their men.

At first my grandfather helped my father with the farm work. I adored my grandfather. I can see him yet sitting in his high straight-backed chair with his big hands resting on the chair's wooden arms. He sat as straight as he walked, his muscular shoulders perfectly horizontal to the chair's back. He breathed heavily, for asthma bothered him. His face was round, his cheeks bright red, eyes small and blue, and his wide mouth was like a new moon turned on its back. Tight ringlets of sandy red hair circled his head. All of his body was built like his shoulders, strong and well proportioned.

He and I, the oldest and youngest on the farm, were friends from the beginning. He was abundantly patient. He let me tag at his heels everywhere. When he went to the barn, I went to the barn. When he came back to the house, I came back too. When in winter he pumped water for the cows, I had to have my hand on the pump handle beside his. When he fed

Grandfather Henry Lape and Mahala Silvernail Lape.

the horses, I gave them my handful of oats. Whenever I was chided for being a nuisance to him, he was quick to defend me. "We're pals," he said, and no words sounded sweeter to me.

He was proud of the two horses, Tom and Jack, that he had brought with him from the Silvernail farm. Tom was a big lanky black, Jack a small fat chestnut. Tom was old, but both of them were nervous high-spirited horses. It pleased my grandfather, on the rare occasions when he went to the village of Esperance, to have them enter town prancing, with their heads in the air. He liked all his animals. Every pig and cow had a name. He sometimes made me jealous when he petted them, for I wanted to be the only sun in his eyes.

He laughed much and heartily. His greetings were always jocular. He read only the daily paper and the monthly *Farm Journal,* in which he liked most of all the series of *Peter Tumbledown* cartoons. He was actively interested in life, but as he saw it himself. His mind recorded the doings of the farm animals, the movements of rabbits and foxes and crows, the changes of weather. He was interested in his neighbors too, but he never gossiped. In spite of his genial disposition he was not a social man. He rarely went to town, and never to any of the communal gatherings like church socials and picnics. He had found in his farm life and his home a self-sufficiency which made his days happy.

Along with his self-sufficiency of mind, he brought with him a self-sufficiency of living which my father was to learn from him. He repaired his own harness, he tapped his own shoes. He butchered all the family meat, cured and smoked hams and bacon strips, put down salt pork, made sausage, headcheese, and liverwurst, tried out lard.

All of the wood ashes were dumped into a big lye barrel, which stood upon a large flat stone behind the house. The stone had three small runnels chipped across it, joining in a slightly deeper runnel, from which the lye water dripped after rains, and was caught. With this soft soap was made.

Soft soap was used for all purposes except washing the face. It was kept in an open nail keg, and out of this some was dipped into another small open keg eight or ten inches high, which always stood beside the sink. Soft soap was the most nauseous looking and smelling substance I have ever known. It looked like snot which had been browned over a fire, and it felt as it looked. I can liken its smell to nothing since. The women always used it sparingly in dishwater lest it scent the dishes.

All farm women in those days baked their own bread

and made their own butter. Both the Silvernails and my grandfather's family had formerly spun their own wool and flax and had the thread and yarn woven into fabrics at a loom in Burtonsville. Now this practice was given up, but Mahala still made all of the clothing for herself and my grandfather: underwear, petticoats, dresses, trousers, nightdresses, and nightcaps. She had never learned to use a sewing machine. She did all of her sewing by hand.

My grandfather always wore too many clothes. In winter both he and Mahala wore red flannel underwear. My grandfather wore them even in summer. Often in hot weather he would come in from work wet with sweat and want a fire built by which to dry himself. In spite of his red cheeks, his circulation was poor. In winter he was always coming into the house and sticking his feet in the oven of the cookstove to warm them. He did this so much that it interfered with my mother's baking. At last my father began building a special fire for him in the parlor stove, an unusual thing, for parlors were closed the year around except for special days.

In the winter over his head he wore a Turkey red hood tied down around his neck and shoulders. An elderly neighbor later told me of my grandfather's once coming for a morning visit in midwinter with his red hood over his head. He found the women in the kitchen sewing carpet rags. He untied his hood, took it off, and sat down. "Get me a needle," he said, "and I'll sew a few carpet rags for you. But mind you don't tell Mahala I did it."

He was a light eater. The Silvernails, who were heavy eaters, thought he never ate enough. He liked sour things, vinegar sauces, plums. Currant pie was his favorite dessert. He liked high spices too. One of the old casters always stood in the middle of the table. It contained, besides the usual salt, pepper, and vinegar, a shaker of cayenne pepper and a bottle of pepper sauce made from tiny red peppers soaked in vinegar.

His only serious physical weaknesses were his asthma and his rupture, for which he wore a truss. I was too young to know what a rupture was, too shy to ask, and nobody bothered to tell me. My grandfather's truss was therefore a tantalizing mystery. I used to see it sometimes hanging over the back of a chair, and it had for me all the fascination of some diabolical machine.

Undoubtedly he influenced me in more ways than I can now trace. I know that it was he who taught me to love crows. Most farmers shot crows, but my grandfather would never let a crow be shot on the farm. "They're our black chickens," he told me. "All they do is get a little corn now and then at planting time, and if we put enough pine tar on the corn, they won't get that. I like to see them around."

We always had plenty of them around, for the farm lay just under one of their daily migration routes. In spring and fall every morning their long flocks straggled up the valley to their feeding fields and every evening back again to the deep pine and hemlock groves near Burtonsville where they roosted. The sound of their calling to each other was as much a part of the daily sounds as the crowing of the roosters in the barnyard.

I was eight when my grandfather died. For weeks afterward I cried myself to sleep at night and then dreamed him alive, holding my hand while we walked through the fields.

After my grandfather died, my father had to hire help. Fred Brown was our first hired man. He was about thirty-five when he came to Oak Nose. His father had been a Methodist minister, by report one of the most brilliant in the conference, but his preferments had always been retarded by the oddity of his family. Fred had inherited his father's brilliance and the family's peculiarity.

He was built like a good fence post, not too tall, thick set but not fat. His head fitted his body, heavy yet compact. His face was long, but squared off tightly across both forehead and jaw. All of his features, and the face muscles themselves, were heavy and coarse. His hands were large and thick fingered. They hung at his sides as if weighted. It seemed as if his body had been given so much weight that it could not hold it all, and the excess had sunk down to his feet. They were tremendous. They planted him flat to the ground as if they had suction cups on the bottom. He walked with them pointed out, and shuffled, so great seemed to be the effort of lifting such weight.

I remember him coming down to the house from the barn with a pail of milk, scuffing those heavy feet over the grass and slopping the milk from the pail. His thick forehead was usually contracted in a frown that pushed his heavy eyebrows together over his nose. His voice was deep and coarse. His favorite expression was a long drawn out derisive, "Aw-w-w-w-w!"

At work he was willing but awkward. He had great strength but never knew how to use it with advantage. And his feet were always in the way. He might tug for fully two minutes at one end of a large flat stone trying to move it. Finally it would dawn on him that both of his feet were planted firmly on the opposite end of the stone. "Aw-w-w-w," he would say, slide his feet back on the ground, and lift the stone. In summer one of his evening jobs was to go out with the team and stoneboat and drag in a load of freshly cut meadow hay for the horses' night feed. He would come down the road with a pile of hay on the stoneboat and himself perched on top of the pile. As the horses swung the stoneboat around the abrupt turn into the driveway, he would roll off and tumble like a huge ball on the grass. "Aw-w-w-w," it would be all over again, while he grinned and picked himself up.

He ate as much as two other men, to my mother's dismay. At meal times those heavy hands would carry both knife and fork to his mouth in a steady delivery. At first helping his plate was loaded like a mountain. He ate everything—meat, potatoes, vegetables, pies and cakes, sweets. He never could get enough meat dumplings. He was always trying to get my mother to make them, even with salt pork. One of the side dishes to all of our dinners was cottage cheese and strawberry jam. Fred would pile on his plate a helping of cheese as big as a fist, and then pour half a cup of strawberry jam over the top of it. And that was only his first helping. My mother had to make a milk pail full of skim milk into cheese every day. He liked his coffee strong. "You can put a pound in a cup for me," he said.

Naturally his digestion suffered. He was always having bellyaches. Then in the night he would take pills, huge pink and white ones. In the dark they would elude his fingers and spill on the floor and roll into the corners of the room.

He was by nature slovenly. Besides the pills on the floor, his room was always a mess of dirty clothes, socks, papers, magazines. His clothes never fitted him, his hair was rarely combed, his hands were usually dirty. He was likewise a careless worker. He had to be watched at any important task.

But the same forces which threw his body so strangely together had done equally strange things with his mind. It was at once brilliant and plodding. A modern psychologist would probably have classified him as one of the higher types of borderline insanity. The Esperance folk merely called him odd. He was a wizard at arithmetic. He could take a column of four digit numbers half a page long and add them in his head before I could even get the first column added. And his sum would be accurate. He was equally quick at multiplication and division. My father, who from his school-teaching days had picked up many short cuts in arithmetic, at first used to try to beat Fred at a sum. But it was like the race of a mule against a Kentucky thoroughbred. Failing so, my father tried to worm out Fred's secret short cuts, but he failed in that too. If Fred knew what they were, he would not explain them. They were probably channels of flow in his mind which made the like thought processes of an ordinary mind seem like dawdling rivulets.

Two things fascinated him above all others, the weather and small intricate machinery. He was always a reader of weather signs. He knew the names of all the various cloud formations. He could detect the slightest change in the direction of the wind. His knowledge of astronomy was immense. He taught me to recognize all the principal constellations, and most of the stars of the first and second magnitude. He had one of the old telescoping spy glasses. Through it I first saw Venus in its phases and the surface of the moon. He always bought the yearly weather almanac published by a Dr. Hicks in Kansas. In these we followed the star maps for each month and traced the changing positions of the planets, which were considered important in weather forecasting. But most exciting in the almanacs were the splendid photographs of storms, brilliant flashes of lightning forked intricately across a black night sky, the great funnel of a tornado advancing toward the observer. It was for these that I loved the almanacs, but Fred followed the weather forecasts religiously. He had his own barometer, an exceptional item for a farm hand or even a farmer of those days to possess. Also he never trusted our thermometer. He put up one of his own.

In his later days at Oak Nose we were crowded for room, and a bed was put up for me in the large room in which he slept. Here on summer nights before we went to sleep, we used to lie, he in his bed and I in mine, and talk about the heavens. He told me about novae and nebulae and star clusters and the formation of new star worlds. It was the first meeting of my mind with the details of outer space. I was fascinated and terrified. Long after Fred was snoring I used to lie awake and look out of the window and sink my mind in that far distant past whose light was just then glimmering through the bedroom window.

Fred's love for small intricate machinery expended itself in the only such things available, watches. He always had three or four, and he was always trading. He took the cheaper ones apart as far as he could with the tools at his disposal. His moment of glory came when he discovered some of my father's watch repairing tools in the spare bedroom and he was finally able to disassemble a watch completely. Of course he couldn't put it together again. Even had he known how, his clumsy fingers would not have done the job. My father helped him with the reassembling. When he saw the watch, that had been a cluster of wheels on the table, together and ticking again, his bliss was childish and pure.

He had an old typewriter, one of the early Hammonds with adjustable type and spring action, that had belonged to his father. He loved to monkey with this as much as he did to type with it. In fact there was little he had to type, except a business letter now and then ordering some new weather almanac or a patent medicine.

Eventually his family needed him and he left us and went back home. But he had become part of our lives, and we missed him at Oak Nose.

Growing up Alone

I grew up an only child, but in this I was an exception among the farm boys of my time. Most of our neighboring families had several children. Five or six was an average number, ten or twelve still reasonably common. Being alone, I learned early how to entertain myself.

The outdoors was my playroom. In the spring I went to the woodlot for mayflowers. Mayflower, that word which varies so with locality, was for us the hepatica. Hepaticas grew in every woodlot. Their dark green and purple three-lobed leaves lay all winter long among the dried leaves under the snow. When the sun drew the sap up the maple trunks, and the leafy forest floor freed of snow breathed with the mellow scent of decay, then the hepatica flowers opened with the morning sun and scented the air. The common colors were white, pale pink, and lavender, but I always looked for the rarer deep blue ones with frosty edges, or the deep carmine ones. I would pick until my fingers could hold no more of the soft furry stems and then take the little bouquet home to my mother.

Once when I was after mayflowers alone in our own woodlot, I got lost. It was an experience I have always remembered. What I remember most vividly was not the fright at

"I grew up an only child, but in this I was an exception among the farm boys of my time." Country lad and cow, Freeville, N.Y., 1906. *Courtesy of the Verne Morton Collection, DeWitt Historical Society, Ithaca, N.Y.*

finding myself in a place where no tree or plant looked familiar, but the moment of finding my way again, when all the strange looking trees and slopes and patches of sky swung into a familiar pattern.

As a child I never came to know wildlife intimately. Men who know it in early life are usually those who have learned it out of necessity. The trapper knows the ways of animals because he cannot catch them without that knowledge. The Indians knew both plants and animals because most of them were either food, medicine, or direction pointers. But the boy who merely observes for his own pleasure observes spottily.

I came to know what my father knew. He knew plants and trees well. I was soon taught to recognize every tree or herb in the woodlot. I went with him in summer to the meadow swales to gather boneset, which he hung in the granary until it dried and then used for medicinal tea. At the right time in spring, when the willow bark would slip easily from the wood, he taught me to make whistles. He did not know birds at all, except the common ones like the robin. All of the many varieties of sparrows were just sparrows to him. And since he never trapped, he knew little about animals.

There was one animal that I learned to know by myself, the woodchuck. Oak Nose abounded with them. Every pasture outcrop of bedrock had a woodchuck hole at the base. In the rich meadows mounds of fresh earth marked burrow doors under the grass. Even in the woodlot they dug under the roots of huge hemlocks. Farmers hated them because a horse or a cow could step into a hidden woodchuck hole and break a leg. So there was always open season on woodchucks. Even my father, who never hunted, shot them. Farm dogs were trained from puppies to hunt them. Nevertheless they survived, because like most rodents they reproduce more rapidly than they can be killed.

My father told me that if I wanted anything to do in my spare time, I could hunt woodchucks. He would not let me use a gun, but he showed me a more primitive way of hunting them, the method that dogs use.

The woodchuck is a wary animal. He depends upon the nearness of his hole for safety. He rarely goes more than a hundred feet from its mouth, and the slightest hint of danger sends him scurrying to it, where with safety accessible he will rise on his haunches and survey the landscape to see just how imminent the danger may be. If the danger seems near, he will retreat into the mouth of the hole but still stick out his head and watch.

If, however, he is by some mischance caught unawares by something between himself and his hole, he will not run away like another animal. He merely flattens in the grass and waits. If he is cornered by a dog or any enemy near his size, he will put up a good fight, but a man can walk up to him and tap him on the head with a stick. He is easily stunned.

My job then was to catch a woodchuck out feeding and get between him and his hole. But a woodchuck is not easily caught napping. He has a keen sense of smell. Always when he is eating, the thin outer skin of his nostrils keeps going in and out for the slightest trace of danger in the air, and like a bird he never feeds long without looking up.

The stalking of woodchucks became my game. I had every hole on the farm charted. I knew how many woodchucks were in each hole, where they fed, and what time of day each one was most likely to be out. I got up early in the morning when the field sparrows were still trilling in the dewy grass. Late in the afternoon, when I ought to have been helping with chores, I was scouting for woodchucks in clover.

But I was young and clumsy. I was no match for the canniness that instinct gives an animal. I would kneel down in the grass and creep over the crest of a knoll, face level with the clover and timothy heads. But always before I reached the top the keen woodchuck nostrils had smelled me, and all I could see was the tip of a brown nose sticking out of the burrow and sniffing the air. I used to carry small stones and aim them at that brown nose, but the woodchucks all made sport of dodging any such slowly moving thing as a thrown stone. The stone would hit the ground, the chuck give a whistle, and the brown head would be gone without my seeing it go. Failing at one home, I would run on to the next, like a dog hunting.

Late one afternoon I caught the big female by the cattail spring in an unwary moment. I came up through the grass behind the spring and her hole. She was contentedly nibbling on the warm slope below the spring. The wind must have carried my scent away from her. I got within ten feet of her hole, and still she had not seen me. I was exultant. I jumped up and ran for the hole. She saw me coming. Either she underestimated my speed or accurately estimated my weakness, for instead of flattening in the grass, she too came straight for the hole, her fat brown body hugging the ground. I stood on the mound of fresh earth in front of the hole and waved my stick. She never stopped. There were six inches of space between my feet, and she went through, gnashing her teeth. Her movement and my fright upset me. I toppled backwards across the hole, but in the half second while I was falling she slid under my body to safety.

This defeat, ignominious as it was, only whetted my eagerness. It made all woodchucks increasingly important. It made stalking them a greater game than ever. I made up little ditties about them, which I sang while I went running through the grass. I talked aloud to myself and to the woodchucks. I told them they couldn't fool me all the time, I'd show them a thing or two.

One day I had been to the hayfield and was returning. I was not even thinking of woodchucks, for it was only midafternoon, not yet their feeding time. I came bursting around the clump of brush by the old stone quarry, close to the burrow of one of the biggest males on the farm. I stopped abruptly. The big fellow himself was grazing down on the slope below the quarry. He had not even seen me, and I was between him and the entrance of his hole.

I was so excited that the skin on my neck burned. I grabbed a piece of dead branch from the brush at the quarry's edge and moved toward the woodchuck. He saw me, and saw that it was too late to do anything. He flattened in the grass like a blob of brown mud. I walked slowly toward him. He never moved. I came close. I raised the stick and whacked him twice over the nose. It was all over. I hit him again a couple of times to make sure, and then I poked his body with the stick. It rolled over on its back, limp. I dropped the stick. I was trembling.

I picked him up by the long bushy tail. He was fat and heavy, and the tail was warm. When I held him up, he was nearly as tall as myself. I had to hold him high so that he would not drag too heavily on the ground when I carried him. I started home. I was excited, proud, uneasy. My great moment had come, but it lacked the satisfaction I had expected.

I dragged the woodchuck down the steep slope and across the road and up the driveway and across the yard to the wagonhouse, where my father was unhitching the horses.

"What you got there?" my father said.

"A woodchuck," I said, as if it were something I brought in every day.

"You sure he's dead?" my father asked.

"Of course he's dead," I said.

"Well, he's moving," my father said.

It was true. The woodchuck was contracting his legs. Now he drew them together, pulled himself over on his belly, opened his eyes, and looked around in a dazed way. Then he began to crawl.

"You only stunned him," my father said. He picked up a stout stick, and walking over, he gave the woodchuck three smart blows on the skull.

"There," my father said, "now he's dead for sure."

I looked down on him. The legs contracted and then stretched out. And then he was still. His small brown nose lay in the manure dirt at the edge of the driveway, and a trickle of blood ran down out of the side of his mouth.

I felt the tears starting warm around the edges of my eyeballs. I turned and went around the corner of the wagonhouse, out past the barnyard and behind the cowstable, and there I bawled. It was a strange victory.

In memory all the Sundays of my childhood were sunny and without wind. No storms ever marred their serenity. The sun rides in luminous haze over the Mariaville hills. The grass is still wet with dew. The cows are grazing in the lush June grass below the barn. A thin pearl mist still lies in the valley over the crick. All the landscape is like a face that has just been washed. Up out of the valley comes the ringing of the church bells, the solemn boom of the Methodist bell and the gayer kling of the Presbyterian bell.

I am sitting in a chair on the stoop at Oak Nose. On the hillside across the road a large woodchuck is nibbling clover. I want to go stalk him, but I don't dare. I am dressed in my Sunday clothes, and my mother has just warned me from the doorway, "Now don't you go playing around and get yourself all dirty before we get ready to go." I don't dare even to sit on the steps. I am stuck in the clean respectability of the chair. I stay there until my father drives Tom and Jack hitched to the democrat wagon down to the horseblock. They shine like the valley, like my clothes. My mother comes out of the house, tucking a last strand of hair under her hat. I follow her down to the horseblock and get into the seat between the two of them. A horseblock was a small platform of stones with two steps leading to its top, upon which one could stand and step into the wagon. A democrat wagon was a shallow rectangular box mounted on light wheels, with a dashboard in front and a waist-high backed seat resting on the side walls of the box. The seat could be slid along the sides to various positions, and some democrat wagons had a second seat which could be placed behind the first. We all sit carefully upright so that we will not muss our clothes. My mother tucks the lap robe around our knees to keep off the dust. We start down the road. The church bells are still ringing. They are the first warning bells. Sunday school will begin in half an hour.

Sunday school began at nine-thirty and lasted an hour.

It was fun. We did not have to sit still. We could talk, we learned stories, we were given pictures. We sang rollicking songs like *When the Roll Is Called up Yonder*. We were given pins to wear on our lapels and books with gold stars for perfect attendance.

Church was another matter. It began at ten-thirty and lasted until the minister got tired of preaching. The first half was not so bad. Then there was singing and standing up and sitting down for responses, and a long prayer during which we kids could wink at each other or make figures of naked legs and bottoms with our handkerchiefs while our parents had their heads bowed. My woe began with the preaching. The air in the poorly ventilated church made me sleepy. I tried to keep my eyes open, but my head nodded. My mother prodded me with her elbow. I jerked my head upright. The light of the sun shone dully through the stained glass windows, all in memorial to somebody. From one opened window came the song of an oriole in an elm branch, and through the opened window and the elm branch I could see one patch of blue sky and a shaft of sunlight streaking down the street. To be out running in that clear sunlight was all the Heaven I asked for. I wriggled and squirmed in my seat. Old Nelse Jones, who sat beyond me in the pew, reached a grimy hand into his pocket and pulled out half a handful of discolored and broken Necco wafers. He put one in his own mouth, and slid two pieces along the seat to me, evidently hoping to keep me quiet. I took the wafers. They were so dirty that I hated to put them into my mouth, but neither did I want to offend Nelse Jones. So I closed my hand over the wafers, raised my hand to my mouth, dropped my hand back to my pocket and deposited the wafers there, and moved my jaws over one another as if I were sucking a wafer. The effort of the deception awoke me. I stealthily drew my father's watch out of his vest pocket and looked at it. He gave me an understanding grin and put the watch back. I drew a hymnal from the rack on the back of the pew in front of me and leafed over its pages.

But the sermon ended at last. Released from the bad air and the semigloom of the church, I stood in the sunshine on the wide stones in front of the church. All the children were there waiting for their fathers to come out from the church shed with the wagons. We felt as woodchucks must feel who come out of their burrows into the sunshine after a winter of hibernation. How pleasantly the birds sang in the elms. How fresh the touch of cool air on our faces. The women stood in groups gossiping. We children laughed and compared Sunday school pins and began shoving each other off the stones on to the grass until some stern voice cried, "Here, you young 'uns, don't you know it's Sunday?"

Although I was allowed to take off my good clothes and put on my old ones as soon as I got home, the tenor of the day did not change with the changes of clothes. I knew it was still Sunday, and I knew what was expected of me. I was not to go chasing all over the place. I was not to make a lot of noise. If we had visitors and there were children with them, we were not to play games. I could sort out my stamp collection. I could look at my picture books. I could lie on the lawn and read my Sunday school magazines. And when I got bored and restless with all that, my mother would say, "Now why don't you just sit down in a chair and rest?"

To sit down in a chair and rest was the last thing in the world I wanted to do. I was young and full of vigor. Every other day of the week that vigor got its release in action. On Sundays it was bottled up for day. The result was always the same. By the end of the day I had a headache.

Actually my parents were not strict Sunday disciplinarians. For their day in Esperance they were liberal. Some children were allowed to do nothing except read their Bibles. A Sunday of peace and rest was a custom which nobody around Esperance had yet begun to question. None of the business establishments, not even Frank Cromwell's ice cream parlor, ever opened on Sundays. One of the Presbyterian ministers used to have his Sunday paper delivered on Monday morning. It is true that occasional farmers took advantage of a sunny Sunday to get some over-ripe crop into the barn before a rain came, but such doings were always talked about in a low voice during the churchyard gossip, and if by chance the barn of one of these farmers was struck by lighting, its burning was attributed to a just act of God.

When I was seven I started going to school. The school was called the Rock Schoolhouse. It was a little red building, sheltered by woodlots, and looking down over the valley and the village. Across one side of the schoolyard a brook, tumultuous in spring, had cut a rocky bed, in which we younger children built stone dams. The toilets, two little buildings looking like smokehouses, stood side by side at the edge of the brook. Though our house was the nearest in the district to the school, it was a quarter of a mile away. Some of the children had to walk at least a mile mornings and afternoons, and nobody ever brought them to school. They walked.

Red was the universal color for country schoolhouses not out of preference but because red paint was the cheapest paint. Most of the farm houses, if they were painted at all, had the three sides visible from the road painted white, and the rear side painted red. Barns were always red. The Rock Schoolhouse had an entrance woodshed and one schoolroom. The room was heated by a low rectangular cast iron woodstove. The children's desks were commercial oak products, but the teacher's desk was hand made, with a small square body and lathe-turned legs. There were desks enough to accommodate about twenty children, but we rarely had more than ten or fifteen. In winter when the roads were drifted shut, some of the children who

First year in grade school.

The Rock Schoolhouse, 1913.

lived farthest away did not come in bad weather, but I usually got there, for I liked school.

Teaching in a district school was no easy job for a teacher. In the first place the teacher was usually janitor and had to arrive early to get the room warm. Some of the older children were usually almost as old as the teacher, so that discipline was always a problem. And the teacher had the children to care for the whole day and might have to cope with such difficulties as a little boy stung by a bee, a little girl picked on by the older girls, the inevitable tattle-tale, the child who had not bathed properly at home, or even the young girl having her first monthly. Merely getting in all the necessary recitations took figuring, for there was usually at least one pupil in each of the eight grades. The fundamentals were taught, and usually taught well: reading aloud, the basic operations of arithmetic, the laws of English grammar and the structure of an English sentence, and the important events of United States history. Spelling bees made spelling interesting. During recesses and lunch hour the teacher often played with the children.

I think that most of the farm children liked school, not necessarily because they like to study, but because they liked being with other children. They liked the games they played. Many of them came regularly at eight o'clock in the morning to have an extra hour of play before school began.

The favorite game was undoubtedly the most dangerous, duck-on-rock. The equipment for the game consisted of a large flat stone, preferably one four inches or more thick, and a small round boulder about the size of a grapefruit that was balanced on top of the flat stone. The child who was "It" stood about twelve feet behind the rock, and the rest of the children stood about twelve feet in front of the rock, each with a choice stone in his hand about the size of the stone on the rock. Each child took a turn in throwing his rock and trying to dislodge the "duck," the stone on top of the flat rock. If a child's stone dislodged the duck, he had to run forward and touch the rock base with either foot or hand before he was tagged by the one who was "It." If he failed, he became "It" in turn. The game could go on indefinitely. Some teachers would not let us play duck-on-rock because children were frequently hit by carelessly thrown stones. But there was nothing in our play more exciting than that mad scramble when somebody knocked the little round duck off its prop, for it was the time for retrieving all of the stones unsuccessfully thrown.

The safer and more commonly played game was keeley-alley-over. The only thing required for it was a soft rubber ball and the schoolhouse roof. All of the children were divided into two sides. A team took its place on each side of the building. Someone threw the ball over the roof, calling "keeley-alley-over!" If anyone on the opposite side caught the ball, he could hold it concealed and tag anybody on the thrower's side who had not finished a complete circuit of the schoolhouse. If a child was tagged, he must join the side of the one who had tagged him. This continued until one side had acquired all the players.

Fox-and-geese, or hare-and-hounds, was another favorite, as it had been for generations. We had a whole countryside of woods and hills and meadows to run over, and we grew clever at putting our chalked directions on trees and stones where they would be allowably visible and yet hard for the pursuers to discover. We delighted in lying perfectly quiet for ten minutes in some heavy hemlock thicket while the pursuers searched for the elusive chalk marks close to us.

There were also other old favorites: tag, squat tag, hide and seek, red rover, cat, snap the whip. The older boys and girls liked to play baseball, and most of the teachers joined in this, but the younger children did not like baseball so well because they were always outclassed and had to endure the ignominy of having easy pitches put to them when they were at bat.

The teachers were as varied as humanity. They were usually girls of about twenty, some good teachers, some poor. In retrospect they seem to me to have been as good as one could reasonably expect, perhaps better. My first teacher, Nellie Podmore, later became superintendent of schools in a large city. She boarded in the village and walked the mile and a quarter to the school daily through fair or stormy weather. She was an excellent teacher. She kept discipline without seeming effort. She made us study and at the same time like her. And perhaps most important of all, she adjusted her teaching to our individual abilities. But so did most of the other teachers. They regarded us not as a mass but as individuals.

Undoubtedly the most distinctive personality among my early teachers was Nellie Gordon. She came from a farm family. She was brilliant, but she had no discipline. It seems to me now that she was always either laughing or crying. When we were good she laughed, and when we were bad she cried. She taught us well when she was able to keep us under control, but often we were too much for her. We talked aloud, we walked in and out as we pleased, at our worst we threw sugar bags full of sand at her. She paid us to be good. She taught us spool knitting to keep us quiet. I still associate with her the tiny rugs we used to make of the coiled worms of bright colored string that came out of the bottoms of the knitting spools. She put on the best Christmas entertainment that the district had ever known. She drilled us for hours marching around the room, singing *Marching through Georgia* and carrying long wands wound with colored crepe paper, with which and under which joined over our heads we did all sorts of figures. She was the best baseball player in the school.

She boarded at our house. In the evening we did our homework on the kitchen table by the side of the kerosene lamp. She was at the time full of ambition and curiosity, and she recognized and appreciated the temper of my young mind. She was then studying algebra, and she taught me the lessons along with her, far ahead of my time to learn it. Sometimes I used to go sound asleep with my head on the table and later wake up and find that she had done all the problems without me and feel mortified and hurt. And in the parlor in the dusk of evenings she played the melodeon for me, and we sang all the old songs, *Darling Nellie Gray, Juanita, Way Down upon the Swanee River*, and her favorite, *Massa's in the Cold Cold Ground*. How we wailed together on that one, with the kerosene lamp flickering on the corner of the melodeon. She taught me first to put my fingers on the right places on the keyboard, and under her limited but enthusiastic training I began a knowledge of music that in later years became one of my greatest joys.

Her algebra never did her any good. She could control her own emotions no more than she could control us children. She fell in love with a clod of a farm youth, married him, and spent her life drudging for him and their children.

The World of Neighbors

When we had first lived in the slab shack in the Silvernail orchard, the neighbors had considered us visitors. But once we were established at Oak Nose, we became a part of the community, subject to certain communal duties, privileged to share communal pleasures. If we did not know what they were, we were told. The first April two neighbors of the Rock School District came. "Road fixing week," they told my father. "Can you bring your team?"

Obviously no refusal was possible, though my father was anxious to get at the spring plowing. He harnessed Tom and Jack, put pickaxe and shovel in the back of the democrat wagon and me on the seat, and we drove off to the meeting place. There Tom and Jack were hitched to one of the old steel road scrapers, a huge flat scoop with two wooden handles, and the men began the laborious task of putting the dirt roads of the district in shape for the summer. Another team was used to plow out the ditches. The men worked with shovels and picks. They cleaned the ditches after the plowing and filled the sinkholes and the deep ruts of the road with stones. With the horse scraper they covered the bare ledges that the spring rains had left exposed on the hills, and on all the steep slopes they built ridges across the road to divert water to the ditches and save the road surface from being washed away. These were locally called "thank-you-ma'ams" from the jolt they gave to the head and neck of anybody driving over them too fast. Finally the men went along with a stoneboat, a flat sled, and picked up whatever loose stones remained in the road. It was a communal service organized only by the farmers themselves. The shoveling away of the winter snow banks in early spring was done in the same way.

Not long after my father's introduction to communal road repairing, my mother was introduced to another community custom. One fine May morning one of our near neighbors drove in our yard on his way to the village.

"If it's all right with you folks," he said, "our family thought we'd all come over and have supper with you tonight."

My mother said yes, it would be fine, but she was a little put out, and she sputtered to Mahala, my stepgrandmother, "They might have waited until we invited them."

"No," Mahala said, "they don't do it that way. Folks on these hills always go visit newcomers right away. They think it's the neighborly thing to do. They'll expect us to go eat with them afterwards."

My mother was still perplexed. "But we haven't a bit of fresh meat in the house, and I don't want to ask Herman to make a special trip to the village right now in the planting season."

"Pull one of the hams out of the brine," Mahala said.

"But they aren't smoked yet. They've only been in the brine a week."

Mahala shrugged her shoulders. "Folks ain't too particular what they have to eat. It's the getting together that counts."

So my mother pulled one of the uncured hams out of the barrel of brine in the cellar, and sawed off half of it. She baked pies and a cake. Mahala opened a couple of the jars of sauerkraut that she had brought along from the Silvernail place. The neighbor family came for supper. They said how good my mother's meal was. Everybody had a good time. My mother was pleased. She said after they had gone, "They do make you feel at home, don't they?"

Of the communal group divisions of the countryside, the smallest and most intimate was the school district. Everybody in the district attended school meeting in the spring. The election of school trustee was an important matter, since the selection of a school teacher for the coming year was left completely to him.

Each school district also had its yearly picnic. The Rock School District picnic was held in a forest grove on the verge of the cliff walls that the Schoharie had cut for its passage a mile above Burtonsville. It was a beautiful spot, but troublesome to the mothers, who were always worrying that their children would get too near the cliff edge and fall over. But it was an event that nobody in the district missed. The farmers came in democrat wagons and buckboards and surreys. They drove a little way into the grove and tied their horses to trees. The picnic was served on long tables set up in the shade. There was always watermelon for dessert. In the afternoon the women sat around the table and gossiped, the older boys and girls went walking down the steep banks to Buttermilk Falls, on a side brook entering the crick, and the men played a little baseball in the open field outside the grove.

Sunday school picnics were bigger events. Both Sunday schools usually joined for these, and they were held in a more open grove near the Esperance railroad station. They drew big crowds. Everybody was welcome to come, and relatives often came from long distances. For these the meal was more elaborate. There would be hot coffee and lemonade, peanuts and bananas, and watermelon. In the afternoon there would be a full-scale baseball game between Esperance and some neighboring town. And always Amie Clayton would be there with his little accordian to play and dance a jig for pennies.

Amie Clayton was one of the best known figures of the countryside. He was always spoken of as "Amie the halfwit" or "Poor Amie." He lived with his mother on an island in the Schoharie at Burtonsville, four miles down from Esperance. A tall gangling man, then in his early thirties, slightly round shouldered, he peddled needles, thread, pins, and a few patent medicines, all of which he carried packed in a small satchel. For all special days such as picnics he carried also the accordian, on which he played and jigged crudely while he played. For this people would throw him a few pennies, which he was never too proud to pick out of the dust.

Part of his half-wittedness was an impediment of speech, not a stutter but a nervous explosion of voice that, after a gathering silence, sent a whole sentence sputtering forth like machine gun fire, in a voice high pitched and nasal. In many ways he was shrewd. In his peddling he usually knew how to get the most out of his customer, and while he talked his eyes were always nervously but actively looking about, observing everything. At every house where he stopped he gathered a brainful of news and gossip to carry on to the next. He also usually managed to arrive at a house just before meal time and be invited to sit down and eat, and he always did without protest.

The boys and grown men too often teased him, asking him to do impossible stunts or mimicking his dancing or his speech, but he rarely became angry, only looked away in the distance as if by doing so he could dismiss the unpleasantness of life. But for the most part he was well treated wherever he went.

Another large annual community event was the harvest home supper. This was held in the Red Men's Hall in late October or November. Tables were set up in the downstairs room, and the sides of the room decorated with corn shocks and pumpkins and tendrils of bittersweet berries. Meat was cooked especially for the event, but the rest of the meal was supplied by the various housewives and brought to the supper often just out of the oven: pans of scalloped potatoes richly browned over the top, pots of baked beans, raised biscuits, cabbage salads, chocolate cakes, banana cakes, cakes with rich cream fillings. Hot coffee was made on the cookstove at the back of the stage and served in big white cups that were heavy enough to break a toe if they fell on one. After the supper the women washed the dishes and gossiped, the boys and girls ran upstairs and played kissing games, and the men went upstairs and played dominoes or cards in the little back room.

But nobody stayed late, for farmers had to get up too early in the morning. By eleven o'clock they would begin to go to the church shed for their rigs. They would drive up to the horseblock in front of the hall, the women would climb in with their empty baskets and dishes, the young would come reluctantly, and the teams would carry them away in the night, the little kerosene lanterns on the dashboards blinking behind the rumps of the horses.

There were also many smaller suppers given by various church or lodge organizations, ice cream socials, pie socials, covered dish suppers, in which each housewife brought anything she felt like preparing, and a unique affair called a box social. For the box social each woman brought a whole lunch in a box. The boxes were given numbers, and each man drew by lot the number of a box, the contents of which he would share with the woman who prepared it. This always produced certain rivalries and discomfitures, for certain boys wanted to eat with certain girls, and there were certain women in the community whose cleanliness was suspect and whose food nobody wanted to eat. So some sly work and some trading usually accompanied the drawing of the lots.

Besides the suppers there were smaller gatherings at the

homes. Large families usually had an annual family reunion. Certain farm activities such as butchering, threshing, and hay pressing usually required exchange help from the neighbors. One of the proudest days of my early years was the day I was sent off alone with the team and an oak rack to help a neighbor in threshing. Often the women went along with the men, to help the neighbor's wife get dinner for the crew. Then the days of exchanging work became also the days of social gossip. Corn-husking bees were just dying out, but quilting bees were still common among the women.

By all these gatherings we soon came to know our neighbors intimately. We knew their houses and they knew ours, the furniture in the rooms, and what each room was used for. We knew their children and their horses and their cows. We knew what their food tasted like and what their voices sounded like.

It was taken for granted that in the greater emergencies help would be given. When someone died, every neighbor went to offer help and to bring some dish of cooked food to keep the household supplied until after the funeral. When a house burned down it was often said that the family ended better off than before, so generous were the neighbors' contributions of furniture, bedding, clothes, and money.

But sometimes help was given when it was neither asked for nor wanted. Such was my mother's effort at the time of the birth of one of the Berkeley's babies. The Berkeleys lived on the road to the village. They had lately moved to the neighborhood. Knowing that Mrs. Berkeley was with child, my mother had my father stop one day on the way home from the village, while she went in to see how things were.

My father and I sat outside in the wagon. My mother was gone a long time. When she came back her cheeks were flushed bright red, as they always were when she was stirred up.

"She had it two days ago," my mother said. "They

didn't have a doctor and she hasn't got any help. She's in bed in the parlor, with the stained bedclothes lying in a heap on the floor, and the other children running around whining. And he's sitting in the kitchen with his feet in the oven reading one of those Daredevil Dick magazines from Cromwells. He says they don't need any help, but they do."

"What are you going to do?"

"I'm going to stay and clean up the house a little and cook them some fresh food. You go on home and come back for me late this afternoon."

She stayed that afternoon, washed the clothes, cleaned the rooms, baked a cake, and got some food ready for their supper. I went back later with my father to get her.

"Well, I didn't get any thanks for it," she said, while she settled herself with a jerk onto the seat of the wagon.

A delicate smile played over my father's lips. "I suppose you gave him a piece of your mind," he said.

"Yes, I did," my mother said. "I couldn't hold in."

"Well, what could you expect then?" my father said.

My mother made no answer. She brooded all the way home.

But there were more tragic times when help was asked for. One day coming home from church we found Maggie T sitting on the horseblock waiting for us.

"Essie is dead," Maggie T said. She had been crying, but she was dressed in a black lace dress and a fancy hat with an ostrich plume. "I was wondering if you folks would take me down to her house. Things have to be got ready for the funeral, and there's all those children to take care of and nobody but poor Ira to do it."

Maggie T was a widow. She lived with her two children beyond our farm. She was always called Maggie T because there was another Maggie in the community with the same last name, and so they were always called Maggie T and Maggie L to distinguish them. Essie was Maggie T's sister, and Ira was Essie's husband. They lived down on the Burtonsville Road, and there were at least half a dozen children, three of whom came to the Rock School.

"Sure," my father said. "Climb in. I'll take you down while Emma's getting dinner."

But my mother, sizing up Maggie T in her finery, said, "I better go along too, just to see what has to be done at the house. Let Freddie get out and Maggie T get in. Freddie shouldn't be going anyway when there's just been a death."

I got out, disappointed, for I had been making eyes in school at Phoebe, the oldest girl. Maggie T took my place on the wagon seat, and they drove back down the road.

When they came back a little later, my mother told me, "You should see the mess the house is in. If I'd known Essie was so sick, I'd have gone down before and helped out. Maggie T might better have gone down before Essie died instead of waiting until now."

"I think she's got her eye set for Ira," my father said.

"Sure," my mother said. "Maggie T never put herself out much for anybody unless there was something to be got out of it. It makes me feel bad, though, all those poor children left that way. We'll hurry with dinner, and then you take me right back down. I'll help Maggie T go through the house. It'll need cleaning from top to bottom before the funeral. And you might as well not plan on doing much farm work until the funeral is over, for the barns are just as bad."

My father grumbled, "Everything always has to happen at the busiest time. Oats need reaping the worst way."

"Well," my mother snapped, "when people die they don't wait for oats to get reaped. It's a sad thing for that family, and we've got to do what we can."

My mother and father spent most of the next three days helping get Essie's house ready for the funeral, helping Ira do chores, and watching over Essie's children. I went along twice, but the Phoebe with the red eyes was not the Phoebe I knew in school, and I was frightened before her and went off to the barn with the boys. But the bustle in the house impressed me, my mother rushing here and there with broom and dustpan, the neighbors coming and going, and Maggie T in her black lace dress talking with everybody in a hushed but conspicuous voice.

My mother contended that Maggie T made more work than necessary because she insisted on getting an elaborate chicken dinner for all the relatives the day of the funeral, when there was already plenty of food that the neighbors had brought in. "Just to impress Ira," my mother said with a toss of her head.

My mother and I stayed at the house after the funeral while the procession went to the cemetery so the house wouldn't be left alone. It was a superstition among many farm families that a house should never be left alone during any important occasion like a wedding or a funeral.

Afterwards my father drove us home, and later still we saw Ira in his rig taking Maggie T back up the hills to her farm.

"Well, there they go," my mother said. "I guess she's got him roped."

But if Maggie T had such dreams, they were not ful- filled. In less than six months Ira himself died, and all the orphaned children were sent to live with a relative in Iowa.

The Village

Our link from Oak Nose Farm to the world was Esperance, the village that lay a mile and a half down in the valley below us. We knew it only as "the village." It was the center of the life of all the farms that lay along this wide curve of the Schoharie, not only on the valley sides but on the plateaus at their tops. The village was older than most of the farms. It had at first been an inn stop on the turnpike running from Albany to Cherry Valley. This was in the 1700s. Most of the farms, except those along the flood plains, were lots reclaimed from forest during the early 1800s. The strategic position of Esperance, both on the Schoharie and on the Cherry Valley Turnpike, had given it some importance, and it was the first incorporated village in Schoharie Country. By the middle of the 1800s it prided itself upon being the home of the county's intellectual elite, having besides other things furnished a man for the United States consular service. But the building of the Delaware and Hudson Railroad, which slightly bypassed the village, sharply lessened stagecoach traffic on the turnpike, and the village began to stagnate.

However, it was at the turn of the century a beautiful and picturesque village. It lay nestled in the curve of the

Schoharie, with hills rising gently around it. Its streets were lined with elms twice as tall as the two-story houses. Its most distinctive landmark was the covered wooden bridge over the Schoharie. Though the Schoharie is called a creek on the maps, it would in any more arid climate be called a river, and was in 1900 as large as any of the rivers of California except the Sacramento and the San Joaquin. The bridge that crossed it was one of the best built and most interesting covered bridges in the eastern United States. A three span structure, it dominated both the village and the countryside by its sound, for its loose plank roadway was always rumbling with the passing of wagons, audible for miles in the hills.

The houses of the village were clean and pleasant looking, but their architecture was not impressive. A few had the fine proportion and the finish of doorways and windows and cornices that had come from Georgian England, but in most of them the Dutch influence prevailed. They were built close to the street, usually with their gables on the street, and whatever distinction they possessed was apt to be in the lace woodwork of their later added Victorian porches.

Nor did the churches have the beauty of the churches of a New England village. The largest, the Methodist church, was a wooden structure, too boxlike and solid in proportion, and its tower too wide at the base and too heavy. It had a fairly good bell in its belfry, deep toned, and its ringing was always the dominant sound in the valley on Sunday mornings. The Presbyterian church was more imposing, and was, except for the old decaying Academy building, the only stone building in the village. It was a well-built structure, but also both in body and belfry a little too squat and solid. Its interior was more beautiful than its exterior, for it had a balcony supported by columns, and the woodwork of both the balcony and of the pulpit-choir section was well carpentered. The bell was smaller than the bell of the Methodist church, and more soprano in tone. The voices

The covered wooden bridge in Esperance carried the warning: "Take notice: ten dollar fine for any person driving his horse or team faster than a walk over this bridge." *Courtesy of the Esperance Historical Society and Museum*

of the two together were like the voices of man and woman talking.

Main Street was the axis of the village. It began off the end of the bridge as a right angled turn and widened there into a small triangle, in the center of which was a plot of grass, one elm tree, and at the base of the elm tree a small pyramid of black cannonballs, remnants of the Civil War. From this triangle the street ran west, wide and open, to about the middle of the village, where it divided into two roads, with a narrow park down the middle in which were three tall elms and two more

Schoolhouse and Presbyterian church, Esperance, N.Y. *Courtesy of the Esperance Historical Society and Museum*

piles of the black cannonballs. Along either side of the street great elms lifted their boles and swung their limber crowns over the bluestone pavement and the house roofs.

Besides Main Street, which ran the length of the village, there were two other streets, one running north opposite the end of the bridge, and the other cutting across Main Street just beyond the middle of the village, running from the Presbyterian church down to the crick. One narrow street running parallel to Main Street joined these two to form a block. This street in my childhood was known only as The Block. The other streets had the names of Charleston Street and Church Street, but they were never called anything but the Back Street

Tree-lined and divided Main Street, Esperance. *Courtesy of the Esperance Historical Society and Museum*

and the Front Street. Also the Front Street changed its name after it crossed Main Street, like the streets of many Mexican cities, and the section from Main Street down to the crick was called Crick Street.

The Presbyterian church was set on a hill exactly in the middle of Front Street, and the street diverged by a narrow section of road around it. Just below the church was the village school, a one-story wooden structure, and across the street from it was the village green, or commons, no longer put to any use, nor at that time kept in good shape.

The buildings on the east side of the crick, though they lay in Schenectady County, were considered part of Esperance.

Main Street, Esperance, looking west, left, and looking east (c.

They consisted of a grist mill, an old hotel, of which only the saloon was in operation, an Episcopal chapel, and a few houses.

This was all there was of the village. Its population was about 250. But actually the village could not be separated from the countryside about it. Its life and the lives of the farmers on the hills were one. The profits of the farms were the blood that sustained the village. The farmers and farmers' wives made up the body of the churches and the lodges, which were the social forces of the village. There was neither financial nor social distinction between the village dwellers and the farmers. They were all one community, with the village as the center.

This was the village of my earliest memory. I was of the hills, timid and ignorant. The years would change me, as they

1890), right. *Courtesy of the Esperance Historical Society and Museum*

would change my mother and father. Equally they would change the village, sometimes for the better, more often for the worse. But they were changes that most villages of central and eastern United States underwent during the first half of this century.

In those early years going to the village was an event. I was always dressed up for the occasion, and my mother would put on her lace dress with the puffed shoulders and one of the large hats then in fashion. My father always shined Tom and Jack, the two horses. He hitched them to the democrat wagon and drove them down to the horseblock at the side of the driveway. There was always a moment of exasperation at the horseblock for Jack never wanted to stand still, and my mother being timid always let two or three chances be wasted before she stepped gingerly into the wagon. But finally we would all be in, I in the middle, and Tom and Jack would start off on a trot down the road. I continually wanted to grab the whip out of the socket and flick it, but my father was adamant against this. "Only little boys whose fathers drive plugs can play with whips," he said.

In the village we drove first to the Methodist church shed. Each of the churches had a large shed which the farmers used not only during Sunday services, but whenever they came to the village to shop. Each farmer had his own favorite stall and was discomfited if he arrived and found another rig in it. The hand-hewn beams of the sheds were covered with advertisements of Hood's Sarsaparilla and Kendall's Spavin Cure and somebody's Balm of Gilead. My father put halters over the horses' headstalls and tied them to the tie rings on the walls. Then we went to the stores.

My father would be carrying a jar or two of freshly made butter or a crate of eggs to be traded against the groceries. There were three grocery stores in the village, and though they varied in size and arrangement, they were much alike. Each had its big red coffee grinder with a large wheel and foot treadle; a barrel of mackerel in brine; a barrel of molasses bunged and on its side — the story went that the body of an infant had once been found in the bottom of one of these barrels — tea and coffee and spice canisters, all painted bright colors, often with pictures of palm trees or Turkish beauties on the sides; a box of dried herring on the grocery counter; bolts of colored worsteds and linens and cottons stacked on the shelves behind the drygoods counters; a spool case with glass front and rows of spools of colored thread lying like flowers under the glass; needles, pins, shears, cards of fancy lace edgings and ruchings, and cards of buttons. The store counters were heavy wooden planks about a yard wide, worn smooth with years of goods shoved across them.

The post office and Grantier's Store, Esperance, N.Y.
Courtesy of the Esperance Historical Society and Museum

Most of the ready-made goods were men's work clothing, overalls, work shirts, and underwear. Women's dresses,
except for the then universal work dress called a wrapper, were
made either by the housewives themselves or by the local
dressmakers, of which there were always two or three going
from house to house and relaying all the village gossip as well as
making clothes. The stores carried shoes for the whole family,
rubber boots for working in the fields in wet weather, and felt
boots, which both the farmers and their wives wore in the
winter. The felt boots came to just below the knee, and were
worn with ankle high rubber overshoes, which were put on for
outdoor wear but taken off upon entering the house. Felt boots

were an excellent protection against the cold and draughty floors of the houses. Even some of the village people wore them, for at that time there were only half a dozen houses in the village that had furnaces. Wood was the common fuel for stoves, and the fires went out at night except on very cold nights, when they were kept over by large chunks of wood.

There was one hardware store, run by the roofer and solderer, but the grocery stores too kept some hardware, a few pots and pans, nails, coiled cylinders of rope for clotheslines or for the farm hayforks.

Somewhere near the back of the store would be a large potbellied stove, a bench or two, perhaps a few wooden chairs, and a spittoon. In winter there would usually be a group of men sitting about the stove, talking politics, gossiping, smoking, and spitting. A few came often to escape the shrill tongues of their wives.

In the earlier days of Esperance the grist mills might have been considered its economic heart, but by the turn of the century their importance had begun to decrease. Flour was still the chief food of the community, but the ease of railway transportation had already started the trend to centralized production that was to accelerate so rapidly in the twentieth century. Wheat flour was no longer ground in the village mills but in larger mills in the more industrialized sections of the country. It came by freight to the village, and every household had its flour barrel.

But the grist mills were still of prime importance, for each farm in the valley raised all the grain necessary for the feeding of its animals, and much of this grain was taken to the mills to be ground. Buckwheat pancakes were made in every household, and all the buckwheat flour was ground in the local mills from locally raised buckwheat. Also one of the mills, to make up for its decreasing trade, had added a sawmill which operated in the winter and a cider mill which operated in the

One of Esperance's two mills on the Schoharie. *Courtesy of the Esperance Historical Society and Museum*

fall. Most families still made their own cider and their own vinegar. The poorer apples were brought to the cider mill in the fall, and the juice was carried home in barrels to be stored in the cellars over the winter.

There were two mills in the village, one on each side of the crick. Both had once been run by waterwheels, but the waterwheel of the mill across the crick had been replaced by a steam engine, and the one on the village side by one of the huge new gasoline engines.

The mill on the village side was the older and more interesting of the two. It was a large three-story structure leaning slightly over the crick bank. An iron fence paling ran along the edges of the roof, and in the center of the roof was a cupola with an iron weather vane. At the center front of the building was a narrow loading platform up to which the teams were driven to deliver the grain to be ground. Over the platform rose a tier of doors, one in each story of the building, and from a beam projecting at the roof hung the tackled rope by which bags of feed or flour were let down from above and bags of grain carried aloft.

On one of our first visits to the mill, my father took me to see the old waterwheel. It was under the present sawmill. My father took me firmly by the hand. We picked our way along the sawmill track until we came to a little door. My father opened the door. We stuck our heads inside and looked down. A tumbling stone stairway sank into an awful space. Out of the space rose the sagging old waterwheel. At its bottom the water ran dark and silent. A black snake six feet long swam across the water's surface. I cried and pulled my head back out of the doorway.

Upstairs inside the mill everything was noise and dust. Small hoppers buzzed, huge grinding stones turned with a continual heavy crunching, belt conveyors hummed up and down square wooden chutes carrying the grain or the flour or the ground feed to their respective bins. White dust was everywhere, the atmosphere shone with it, the millers were covered with it, all the windows and woodwork were white with it.

More than the mills, I enjoyed Frank Cornell's blacksmith shop. Blacksmithing was important in the village's economy. Frank Cornell's shop was close to the mill and was as black inside as the mill was white. The walls, the tools, the windows were covered with soot from the forge. Frank in his leather apron would hold a horse's hoof between his knees, pare down the hardened and broken cuticle, and fit a new shoe to the hoof. Then he would put the shoe into the glowing coals of the forge, turn the handle of the blower until the whole shoe became red hot, take the shoe from the forge with a pair of tongs, slap it on the anvil, and with a heavy hammer pound it to the desired shape, while the sparks flew from the pounding and the pling of metal against metal filled the air. Then he would plunge the hot shoe into a bucket of water, steam would rise with a burst, and afterwards when the shoe was held to the horse's hoof, the smell of scorched cuticle and manure would fill the shop.

On Main Street at the corner of the alley which led down to the blacksmith shop and the mill was Cromwell's ice cream parlor. The Cromwell house, in good condition, stood on the corner. The one-story shop which adjoined it had with time sagged away from the street until it looked ready to collapse with a good push. In front of the shop hung a square lantern with four sides of red glass, with letters reading ICE CREAM on two of its sides. On summer days a parrot in a cage often hung beside it, and on the walk before the door were two oleanders in tubs.

Frank Cromwell ran the shop. He was one of the main village gossips and always tried to ferret out information from everybody who entered. "I hear there was some sort of trouble at Cy Walsh's yesterday," Frank would say, raise his eyebrows nervously, and wait for a new version of the trouble. He also delivered newspapers throughout the village, prayed aloud in the Epworth League service of the Methodist church for twenty minutes at a time, and kept the walls of the shop lined with lurid Daredevil Dick magazines. In a glass covered counter were chocolate drops, peanut brittle, hoarhound drops, cinnamon drops, birch drops, and gum drops, all in separate trays. These were weighed out on the scales on the counter. In the front window was a peanut roasting machine. There was only one small table in the shop, and this was used only by those who wanted a birch beer, a root beer, or a sarsaparilla.

Ice cream was served by Mrs. Cromwell in a narrow room behind the shop and at a lower level. One ducked his head under the low doorway and descended to sit at a dining room table covered with white oilcloth. In the center usually stood a bunch of flowers, a pitcher of water, some tumblers upside down, and a glass spoonholder full of spoons. The ice cream was made by Mrs. Cromwell herself in a large freezer cranked by hand and packed in ice and salt. The village women often claimed that Mrs. Cromwell watered her milk in making the ice cream. She was, however, a hard working woman, for not only did she make and serve ice cream and take care of her house, but she also ran a small sewing shop in an extension behind the house where a few village women sewed cut-out underwear, later shipped to the city. And neither by her ice cream nor by her shop did Mrs. Cromwell ever get rich.

In the stagecoach days Esperance had had two hotels, but now the change to railroad travel had eliminated the need of more than one. This was the Chapman House. It stood in the very middle of the village, shaded by a magnificent old elm growing at one corner. It was a two-story building with a full height porch running all the way across the front supported by square wooden pillars. The porch came to the sidewalk. Only a low railing running between the pillars made a division line between porch and street. The Chapman House still took summer boarders, but its transient trade was declining, and its main support came from the saloon and the two pool tables in the saloon. The smell of beer always came from the saloon door, and often on the porch the more disreputable loungers of the village would be sitting, smoking and spitting toward the sidewalk. Or perhaps old Doc Marsh, retired, would be slouched in a chair, dead drunk, snoring, his feet resting on the porch railing.

Near the middle of the village there was a drugstore, but it was declining because the local doctors usually supplied the medicines for their patients, and an increasing number of patent-medicines could be bought at the grocery stores. There was also in the village one harness shop, one shoe repair shop, one marble shop, and a butcher shop run by the owner of one of the grocery stores. At one edge of the village there was a livery stable, where summer visitors could rent a horse and a buggy or a team and surrey.

Two other buildings were of social importance to the village. One was the fire hall. On the ground floor stood the small fire engine which threw water by the hand power of a group of men standing on each side of it and pushing up and down two long wooden bar handles. The only water supply for the engine came from four wells spaced down the main street. On the second floor of the fire house that was a long narrow room that had formerly been the meeting place of the Good Templars, the temperance organization so popular in the late 1800s. The Esperance Good Templars had disbanded, and the room was now used for band practice and sometimes for small private parties.

The other building was the Red Men's Hall, the largest building in the village, next to the churches. The Red Men's lodge was then at the height of its vigor, and the building was a new two-story wooden structure. The downstairs room had a narrow stage at the far end, with a cook stove, a sink, and dish closets back stage. On the main floor there were sets of six wooden chairs fastened together as a unit, and with these the room could either be set up as a theatre, or the chairs could be shoved back against the walls to leave the floor space free. Here long stretcher tables could be set up on jacks to fill the floor for suppers. Upstairs were the lodge rooms, one large room with a good dance floor and a small dais for the lodge ceremonies, and a smaller room used both as a cloak room and a place for playing cards and dominoes. The Red Men's Hall was really the village's social center. It was used not only by the Red Men, but was rented for medicine shows, election rallies, dances, harvest home suppers, church donations, Fourth of July ice cream socials.

Another gathering place in the village was the barber shop, run by Ave Vunck. My hair, like that of most farm boys, was cut at home, but my father went every so often to have his hair cut and his beard trimmed. On the shelf in front of the barber chair was an open wall rack, on the shelves of which stood the individual shaving mugs of the principal men in town, usually with the name in gold letters on the mug and a private shaving brush inside. Ave Vunck was an avid fisher and hunter, as well as barber, and the walls of the shop were hung with guns and large calendars with hunting scenes, and at one side was a small glass covered case with fish hooks, lines, reels, sinkers, and ammunition for guns. Toward the back of the room was the usual potbellied stove and wooden benches and spittoon, and here even more than at the stores was the gossiping center for the men of the community.

Sometimes instead of going the rounds of the shops with my father, I stayed with my mother. To her the village was home more than the farm, for she had been born and brought up in it. We usually went first to the house of her sister May, wife of the local hay dealer. May was already in the first stages of tuberculosis, or consumption as it was then called, the disease which was the scourge of the countryside. My cousins, Oscar and Gertrude, older than I, had a pony and a cart, in which sometimes I was taken for a ride. In their house there was one of the new Victor talking machines with a metal horn and cylindrical records, one of which I particularly liked, a xylophone solo of the *American Patrol March*.

Best of all I liked to go with my mother when she visited Mrs. McCarty. Mrs. McCarty had come from the South after the Civil War, and still spoke with a soft southern accent. Her husband, Duke, was both cobbler and harness repairer and had his shop in a small building beside the house. The house was small, and it always seemed full of sunshine and flowers and knicknacks. Mrs. McCarty was a short gossipy woman who had a bouncy way of bobbing around in her chair when she talked, with her chin always tilted up. She had three daughters, two married and in their own homes. The third, Abbie, was a spinster. She was working then as a clerk in the post office and always wore gauntlets there, perhaps to keep her hands from contamination by the mail. She was already the dominant force in the household. She loved flowers. All summer the yard was full of blossoms. It was there from Abbie that I learned to recognize asters and snapdragons and petunias and stock. It was there on midsummer afternoons that I first came to know the odor of perennial phlox, that sweet perfume that still epitomizes an era for me.

Rolling furrows, 1906. *Courtesy of the Verne Morton Collection, DeWitt Historical Society, Ithaca, N.Y.*

The Hard Years

*I*n those early years at Oak Nose my father had to learn the severity of farm life. Most of the farmers of the countryside were up by five in the morning. Six was late. In winter if you looked out of an east window on a dark morning you could see the lights from kitchen windows across the valley gleaming like stars, and if you watched longer you might see the smaller shaking light of a lantern carried from house to barn. The cows were all milked and the animals fed before the families had breakfast.

Spring work began with the removal from outside the stables of the huge manure piles that had accumulated during the winter and the spreading of the manure over the fields that were to be plowed. At the same time came the repairing of fences, resetting posts of the wire fences and tightening the wires that had sagged from snow, resetting corner poles for the few remaining rail fences, and relaying sections of stonewall that the frost had heaved apart. I liked to help with this and started my own little section of wall, and according to my grandfather, when he offered me a few suggestions, I retorted, "Now don't go butting in when I'm working."

I also liked to help clean stones from the plowed fields.

Tom and Jack were first hitched to the stoneboat and then loose stones piled on it and dragged to the nearest stone pile, mounds scattered on the fields like Indian cairns. A stoneboat, always homemade, was an essential farm conveyance. Every farm had one. It was a flat wooden sled, without runners, usually about six feet long and five feet wide, with some sort of a hitch on the front to which the whipple-tree could be attached. The whipple-tree, also a useful farm tool, was a double section yoke to which the traces of the harness of the horses could be attached. The stoneboat had no box or side boards. Originally designed to collect a load of stones from the fields after plowing and to carry them to a stone dump pile, it was used for transporting almost anything heavy, because it saved lifting a heavy article onto a wagon or high sleigh.

It was not picking up stones that I liked, it was riding on the stoneboat, which was forbidden during stone loading. However, I used to sneak a little ride on a corner now and then, and like a rooster crowing, I could never resist exulting afterward. Another of my grandfather's stories was that once I tried to sneak a ride just as the horses were starting. The horses lurched swifter than usual, and while I shouted in triumph, "See, I'm riding!" the stoneboat slid out from under me and left me flat on my bottom on the wet ground.

Once the fields were plowed, cleared of stones, and dragged, they were planted with the first crop of the season, oats. The oats were broadcast by hand. Mechanical drills had not yet appeared. Rural landscapes have lost a thing of beauty since grain ceased to be broadcast by hand, for the motions of a man sowing were inherently graceful.

As soon as the oats were sown, the land that was to be planted in corn had to be plowed, cleared of stones, dragged, and marked for planting by a sled made of a long plank with four or five pegs projecting downward at regular intervals along its base. Corn was planted by hand, with a hoe. The corn itself,

Farming was a demanding, strenuous life. Ray Morton hoeing potatoes, 1906. *Courtesy of the Verne Morton Collection, DeWitt Historical Society, Ithaca, N.Y.*

coated with pine tar and flour to keep off the crows, was carried in a shallow sack tied around the waist. This was one of the first farm chores in which I was allowed to help. My father planned to have the corn planted by Memorial Day, and the old saw for good growth was, "Corn knee high by Fourth of July." Pumpkins were always planted with the corn. The last crop was buckwheat, not planted until the first of July since it grew and matured quickly. But by this time the corn was ready to be cultivated and hoed.

Haying was the most strenuous work of the year. Then all the family — men, women, and children — were called into service. As soon as I was old enough to drag a hand rake over the ground, my task was to follow behind the men pitching on a load and to rake up their leavings into piles. My mother drove the horse rake in the fields and drove the horses for the hay fork at the barn, while my grandfather on the load set the fork, and my father mowed away the hay in the hayloft.

Men were proud of good hay and treated it and cured it carefully. The grass was cut, left a day to wilt in the sun, raked up, stacked by hand in small cocks, left to cure in the cocks for a day or two, safe from rain, then opened up for a final drying, pitched on to the hay wagon, and carted to the barn. All this required constant hand work. Weather was a continual worry. Men scanned the skies for signs of rain as they might watch a face for moods of temper. Should a thunderstorm loom in the west, the hay rake would go rattling back and forth across the field, and the men would hurry along after it, rolling the windrows into cocks, or pitching the hay on the hayrack feverishly, always watching the progressing storm. How many times I have stumbled along behind the finally loaded wagon, the horses trotting with it, the load jolting over the earth, and pulling in upon the barn floor just as the first drops of rain came spattering down on the barn roof.

After haying came the harvesting of the crops, first the oats, and later, just before frost, the buckwheat and corn. Oats and buckwheat were reaped and threshed as soon as dry, and since threshing required more help than the average household possessed, farmers always exchanged work at this time. Corn was cut by hand and tied into shocks to dry. Sometimes the shocks were left standing in the field and the corn husked there,

Mrs. Will Graves loading hay, a seasonal task which called the whole family into service. *Courtesy of the Verne Morton Collection, DeWitt Historical Society, Ithaca, N.Y.*

sometimes they were stored on the barn floor and husked later during the winter.

There was no more pleasant time of year to my father than late autumn, when all his crops were harvested. His mows bulged with hay. The granary bins were yellow with grain. There was a mow full of oat straw with which to bed down the stock. On the barn floor shocks of corn stalks, stripped of their ears, waited to be fed to the cows. Outside the barn the slatted corn crib was full of ears of orange corn. No worry about feed for the stock, however bad the winter. The emergencies were prepared for. He could meet the cold with a feeling of security for himself and for his stock.

My mother was not so happy, because butchering time was ahead. My father and my grandfather did all their own butchering. Pork was the most common meat. Hogs were scalded in a huge cast iron kettle heated over an open fire. On the actual butchering days neighbors often exchanged help, for the scalding of a three-hundred-pound hog took muscle. The meat to be used during the winter was allowed to freeze, wrapped in newspapers, and packed in barrels. The hams, shoulders, bacon slabs, and hog belly fat were put down in brine and later smoked, except the fat, which was kept in the brine as salt pork. Some of the scrap meat was ground up into sausage. The fat scraps were tried for lard, the head was boiled for headcheese, the hocks were pickled, the liver was made into liverwurst.

To me as a child, one of the joys of butchering was getting the pig's bladders, which when dried made fine balloons that crackled at each touch. Beef was either frozen, or preserved as dried beef or corned beef. Veal was used up quickly during freezing weather, or canned.

Most of the afterwork of butchering fell upon my mother. She did not enjoy it, nor did she like the smells with which it filled the house. And there was another smell which at the same time made the house unpleasant, the smell of crocks of cut cabbage fermenting into sauerkraut.

Nevertheless, when winter came we were ready for it. The cellar was full of barrels of apples and barrels of potatoes and carrots and beets, and jars of canned fruit and canned vegetables and pickles. There was a barrel of flour in the pantry, and buckwheat flour ground from our own buckwheat, and crocks of butter from our own cows, and daily their milk and their cream. Whatever came we would be well fed.

Barrelling apples, 1906. *Courtesy of the Verne Morton Collection, DeWitt Historical Society, Ithaca, N.Y.*

For me winter meant riding downhill. At first I had a little wooden sled, handmade but with iron runners fashioned by the local blacksmith. I always rode it flat on my stomach— we children called it going bell-woppers—but unless the snow was hard it was not very fast, and I was always wearing out the toes of my overshoes trying to steer it. Next my grandfather taught me to take an old dishpan, sit in it with my arms and feet projecting, and go sliding willy-nilly down an ice-covered field. It was actually slower than my sled but exciting because of the unpredictability of direction. Then finally I was given one of the new flexible fliers, that one steered by twisting the thin steel runners by a bar in front pivoted at the center. On hard snow or ice this was very fast, but I still wore out the toes of my footwear for the hand steering was never fully successful on turns.

For me winter was the happiest time of the year, and it should have been for my father and mother, for once the butchering was over and the meats put away and the sauerkraut stored in the cellar, no longer stinking, work eased. Unfortunately, midwinter was the time the interest on the mortgage came due. My father was not yet worried about it, but my mother, lonely on the farm, imprisoned in the house now by bad weather with Mahala to irritate her, and pessimistic about the future, was often unhappy and morose, and her dissatisfaction clouded the household.

In fact, it was soon obvious that the household was going to be plagued by discontent. My mother had not been used to farm life, and she never would get used to it. Its rewards did not seem to her to compensate for the hard work and the loneliness.

The basic trouble was that the hilly acres of Oak Nose were too lean to produce abundant crops. Too much of the land was good only for pasture. Working hard from daybreak until dark, my father could obtain only a modest living. There was money for the necessities, but at the end of the year there was always that interest on the mortgage to be paid, that sixty dollars that never seemed to be there. It was the grim shadow over the door.

"If only we didn't have that mortgage," my mother would say wearily.

"Someday," my father would say, smiling.

While my genial grandfather lived, he was able often to smooth over the rough edges. When he died, Mahala went back to live with her sisters on the Silvernail farm. At first my father was relieved to be free of the household friction she had caused. But he soon found that the three aging Silvernails were adding more responsibilities to his already overburdened days.

For the Silvernail sisters, united again, it was probably the happiest time of their later lives. They were the remnant of a closely united family. Their father, Coonrad Silvernail, had bought the farm from its original grant in the middle of the century and himself cleared it from forest. There was a son who had early left the homestead and settled in Connecticut and a fourth younger sister who had married a man in Burtonsville. Coonrad and his wife, and Maria, Jane, and Mahala formed the home family unit. Maria, the oldest, was never called anything except M'ri, pronounced *Muh-rye*. I cannot discover that either M'ri or Jane ever went out much with boys, and Mahala was past middle age when she married my grandfather and never had children by him. There may have been some connection between this intense family feeling and the fact that Martha, the youngest sister, who had married and left home, hanged herself when she was only twenty-six.

Coonrad Silvernail must have been a thrifty farmer, for he left enough at his death for the three girls to get along on for the rest of their lives. They all stayed on the farm. At first they kept their stock and had a hired man. Then my grandfather married Mahala and took over the farm. After my grandfather died and Mahala came back to her home, they let my father use the land in return for watching over them, for they were now all old women.

They had a signal. If they were in trouble, they hung a red rag on the door of the hogpen, which was between their house and the road and plainly visible from the south windows of our farmhouse.

They had always been individuals, never molded into the common cast of their neighbors. They were not bothered by public opinion. They took no newspapers. In the middle of their eighty acres, they lived by and for themselves. When my mother had been engaged to my father, he then living in the Silvernail household, a village woman had cautioned her, "I don't know, Emma. Those Silvernails are different from the rest of us. They keep to themselves."

They were now women of seventy, all of them stocky but not pulpy. M'ri had rheumatism and walked around the house with the aid of a small ladderback chair, which she dragged with her wherever she went. I still have her chair, with one rear leg worn shorter than the others by her years of dragging it over the floor. After we bought Oak Nose farm, my grandfather used to go down with Tom and Jack hitched to the stoneboat, set M'ri's chair on the stoneboat and M'ri on the chair, and so bring her up to Oak Nose for an afternoon visit. But she had not always been so lame. There were stories of how she had once gone hops-picking at Seward and at night on the barn floor had lifted her long skirts above her ankles and danced a jig that made the floor rattle. In her old age she was a commanding-looking woman. She was the stoutest of the sisters, but she held her flesh well. Her features were pretty, although small for her face. She had a small mouth that curled nicely in a laugh. But she was spunky and quick to show her temper when displeased. So there were frequent periods when she and my mother scarcely spoke to each other.

Jane was the tallest and best looking. Her hair was light and hung in long tight curls over the sides of her head. She was the liveliest of the lot, always jolly, and for a while after Mahala married my grandfather, she left the farm and went to live in the village. She did not work. In fact, she had money enough of her own to buy a house in the village. The villagers said she was a little odd, but she was so gay they couldn't help liking her. Evidently village life did not please her, for in a few years she sold her village house and came back to the farm.

My earliest memories of their house are from the time that M'ri and Jane were living there alone. I can yet see the black vase of twisted paper spills sitting on their parlor mantel. Spills were tightly rolled sheets of newspaper about a foot long. They were used for lighting pipes and all sorts of fires to save matches. None of the Silvernail sisters smoked, although many of the old women of the countryside at that time did smoke pipes, usually clay. The Silvernails used the spills for lighting their candles and kerosene lamps. They lifted a stove lid and held the spill inside until its end lighted. The same spill could be used many times until it burned too short to be held comfortably.

I remember too most vividly the homemade fly traps which in summer always sat on the window sills. They were made from a glass tumbler and a piece of cardboard. The cardboard had a small hole cut out in the center and was laid over the top of the tumbler. Soapy water was put in the tumbler and molasses rubbed on the under side of the cardboard. These flytraps came next to soft soap in my knowledge of nauseous looking things. The sides of the tumbler were stained. In the viscous gray liquid flabby dead flies floated. Live flies buzzed frantically in the small space between the water and the cardboard.

The furniture of their house, ordinary then, would be very valuable today. There was a cherry six-legged table with leaves that nearly touched the floor. There were Boston rockers, Windsor chairs, pine chests and cupboards, maple cord beds, rush bottom ladderback chairs, quantities of blue and pink Staffordshire ware, and a complete set of sheaf-of-wheat ironstone china. All of their teacups were of the type without handles. Their dining room table was an early handmade extension table. Its top was of cherry that had been sawed out of their own woodlot, its legs curly maple.

I remember them always sewing carpet rags. All old bright colored clothing was cut into long narrow strips. The strips were sewed end to end and wound into huge balls. When several bags of balls had accumulated, they were sent across the valley to Mrs. Young, a farm woman who had a carpet loom in her kitchen. Mrs. Young wove the rags into yard wide lengths of carpet, either in a hit-and-miss pattern or in stripes. For a large room these lengths were sewed together into a carpet that completely covered the floor. The floor was first covered with a thick layer of oak straw and the carpet then stretched tightly over that and tacked down at the edges. Short lengths of the carpet were used for throw rugs in the pantry, halls, and smaller bedrooms.

The three old women lived in the same house and ate at the same table, but each kept her own larder and cooked her own food. Their separate larders were not, I think, caused by niggardliness, although they were all saving, but because each preferred to have her own taste satisfied. They loved to eat. They were always talking about what they were going to have for the next meal. Each catering so to her own separate taste, they lived with little dispute. What one did not like, another did. M'ri and Mahala scorned eating their ham and bacon rinds. They gave them to Jane, who relished them fried crisp.

They were continual tea drinkers. Each had a cup of tea always on hand. They kept the same grounds in it all day, left it sitting on the back of the cookstove, and as they drank the tea off, added more water from the teakettle.

M'ri was a great knitter. Although by my time they no longer spun their own wool and flax, they still had fat bolts of yarn packed away from the earlier days, and from these M'ri knit full length stockings for all of them, mittens, and winter wristlets.

Like all women of their time they wore petticoats, in winter so many that they bulged out below the hips like old-fashioned beehives. They never wore drawers, and for some reason prided themselves upon it. In summer Jane would go out in the yard, left up her skirt and petticoat, squat, and urinate.

They had not kept any stock, even chickens, after the time that my grandfather left them. Yet they never wanted for money. M'ri, long before her death, had picked out the clothes in which she wanted to be buried. She got them all out once and showed them to my mother, and gave explicit directions concerning them. "Maybe you think it's funny my talking about such things," she said, "but I don't mind it."

M'ri was the first one for whom the red rag went up on the hogpen door. She died in the night, quietly. She left no will, but there were gold pieces, fives, tens, fifty dollar gold pieces put away for her burial expenses.

After her death Jane and Mahala lived in the house alone. Then Jane began to break up. Her mind weakened. She thought somebody was going to poison her. In her last days she grew helpless, and my mother had to tend her, even feed her.

I remember her death particularly because I saw her embalmed. I was about twelve years old at the time. My father, always curious, wanted to watch, and at my begging must have decided that I might as well see too. In those days bodies were not taken to undertakers' parlors. The undertaker came to the house. Jane was laid out in the Silvernail parlor. I still remember the darkened room, the blood pump, and Jane's withered flesh reviving with the embalming fluid.

Her death was the end of the Silvernail tenure. Mahala took her share of the household things and came back to live with us at Oak Nose, an arrangement not quite happy for her, nor for my mother. The rest of the Silvernail things were sold at auction. I remember in cleaning out the house I came upon a vaginal syringe. I never knew its use, but my mother, coming upon me while I was examining it with obvious curiosity, snatched it from my hands and tossed it into the pile of junk to be discarded.

Entertainment at the Village

*E*sperance was a religious community. Both dancing and card games were prohibited by the disciplines of the Methodist church and of the Presbyterian church. Kissing games were the churches' substitute for dancing. There was, however, a small group of persons who still thought dancing safe entertainment, and for them there were occasionally held bean bakes or gala dances in the ballroom of the Chapman House. The community was divided into two sections, those who considered the dancers at a Chapman House bean bake already on the road to hell, and those who considered the kissing games of the church socials only a milk toast substitute for an ancient pleasure of life.

Since my father and mother were church goers, I belonged in those years to the heavenward bound. All the other boys and girls in our group and I knew exactly what to look forward to when there was a church supper in the Red Men's Hall. At five or six o'clock supper was served in the large room downstairs. We youngsters always liked to eat at the first tables because as soon as we finished eating we could rush upstairs and play. Even while we were grabbing a piece of Sate Easton's banana cake, we had our eyes on the door to the stairway to see if it was yet open. And the moment we had crammed the cake half-chewed down our gullets, we slid off our chairs and ran for the stairway. It was an enclosed wooden stairway, which made the upstairs of the hall a terrible fire trap, but that did not bother us. When we got upstairs there was never any doubt in our minds about the first thing to do. Zadok Brown would grab Olive Jones and link arms with her in the middle of the big room. Olive would shout to Ada Hunter, "Get somebody to catch you, Ada." And then the fun had begun.

Of all our indoor games, catch, the most violent, was always the most popular. It was nothing but a glorified tag with a kiss for the reward of catching. I am not quite accurate. It was a little more than tag, for the person to be caught had not only to be touched but to be held, and that made a great difference. A torn shirtwaist was nothing to the fun of eluding a hand grabbing for a shoulder.

The set-up for catch was simple. A boy and a girl stood with locked arms in the middle of the floor and served as a dodging post for either a boy to chase a girl or a girl to chase a boy. Having started a game, I will finish it. Ada Hunter asked Harry Jones to catch her. She was allowed to use as a buffer anything else in the room besides the standing couple, standing or walking persons, chairs, the piano. A favorite stunt was to grab a section of chairs, which were nailed together in sixes to make long benches, and shove this over the floor in front of the pursuer. If one gave the chairs a jab forward at just the right moment, it was possible to bark the pursuer's shins nicely. When Harry caught Ada, he led her to the standing couple and kissed her. Olive then dropped out of the game. Ada took her place on the floor, linking arms with Zadok, and Harry got a girl to catch him. So the game went on indefinitely with a continual moving up, like scrub baseball. Sometimes there would be three or four sets of catch all going on at once, and any of the runners could use any of the standing couples for buffers. The more runners, the more bumps, and the more confusion, the more fun.

When we had worn ourselves breathless with catch, we would turn to something requiring less effort, one of the singing games. There was for instance *Sailing in the Boat*. In this everybody in the room joined hands and circled. Two or three or four were shoved into the middle of the circle. The circling group sang:

> Sailing in the boat when the tide runs high,
> Sailing in the boat when the tide runs high,
> Sailing in the boat when the tide runs high,
> Waiting for your partner to come bye-and-bye.*

At this point each of the persons in the center would chose a person of the opposite sex from the circle and draw him or her inside. The singing went on:

> Here comes your partner and it's how-do-you-do,
> How have you been since I last saw you?
> How have you been since I last saw you?
> Kiss your partner and say skidoo.

The partners were kissed, the persons originally in the middle returned to the circle, the newly chosen ones stayed in the middle, and the singing went back to the beginning.

If we were very tired, there was another variety of this called *Three Homely Old Maids*. In this chairs were pushed inside the ring, so that those in the middle could sit down. The song went:

*Musical notation for the kissing game songs and square dances described in this chapter are in the Museum of the Esperance Historical Society.

Three homely old maids sat down to sleep,
Sat down to sleep, sat down to sleep.
Three homely old maids sat down to sleep.
        Heigh-O, heigh-O, heigh-O!

They want somebody to keep 'em awake,
To keep 'em awake, to keep 'em awake.
They want somebody to keep 'em awake.
        Heigh-O, heigh-O, heigh-O!

And now they rise just for your sake,
Just for your sake, just for your sake.
And now they rise just for your sake,
        And kiss 'em right under the nose.

There was still another game that offered two kisses instead of one and also gave a chance for amateur acting. The set-up was the same, a group circling with joined hands and a few lone persons inside.

Oats, peas, beans and barley grows,
Oats, peas, beans and barley grows.
You nor I nor nobody knows
Where oats, peas, beans and barley grows.

Thus the farmer sows his seeds,
Thus he stands and takes his ease,
Stomps his foot and claps his hand,
And turns around to view the land.

Waiting for a partner,
Waiting for a partner.
Open the ring and choose her in
And kiss her as she enters in.

Now you're married you must obey.
You must be true to all you say.
Chop her wood and carry it in,
And then she'll let you kiss her again.

Occasionally we played *London Bridge is Falling Down*,
but more frequently we played the same game to another song,
The Needle's Eye, which for beauty of melody had preeminence
among the kissing game tunes.

The needle's eye, it doth supply
The thread that runs so truly.
It's many a lass that I have passed,
      But now I have caught you.

      With a bow so neat,
      And a kiss so sweet,
We do intend, before we end,
To have this couple meet again.

The kisses with which all of these games ended were as
varied as the persons who gave them. Some girls offered only
their cheek, but most took a resounding smack on the mouth
and liked it. There were delicate kisses, bashful kisses, rough
kisses, awkward kisses, but never sensual kisses. They were
given under the full gaze of the crowd, in the yellow glare of the
kerosene lamps, and the blatant kisses of the movies had not yet
been offered as models. It was in the struggle to kiss and to
escape being kissed that the excitement lay. The kisses themselves were anticlimatic.

Some of the games we played were not kissing games at
all, merely singing and running games which involved one or

more persons being forced out of the group by lack of a partner. The most commonly played of these was Pig in the Parlor. In this the couples did a grand-right-and-left in a circle, in which the leftover men, or pigs, joined. At the chorus the men reversed, and when one of the pigs found a girl he wanted, he shouted, "Pig!" The ensuing scramble decided who would be the leftover pigs for the next round. This was the song:

> We've got the pig in the parlor,
> We've got the pig in the parlor,
> We've got the pig in the parlor,
>
> > And that was Irish too-oo,
> > And that was Irish too, oh-h-h,

Another, played in much the same way, except that the circling was done in couples instead of by a grand-right-and-left, was Happy as a Miller, sung to the tune of *Turkey in the Straw*.

> Happy as a miller as he lives by himself.
> As the wheel goes around he's a-gaining on his wealth,
> One hand in the hopper and the other in the sack,
> As the wheel goes around and he cries out
> > GRAB!

Once during the evening we usually did a dance, the Virginia Reel, but we never thought of it as a dance. We called it High-Jim-a-long, and we did it to the tune of the Virginia Reel, but to these words:

High-Jim-a-long, Jim-a-long-Josie,
High-Jim-a-long, Jim-a-long-Joe.
Any pretty girl that wants a beau-sie,
Fall in the arms of Jim-a-long-Joe.

These were the entertainments at large parties, and they kept us amused all evening. Usually toward the end of the evening there would be a revival of catch. The older women would have come upstairs by now, done with washing dishes and gossiping downstairs. We boys always liked to ask some of the fat old ladies to catch us. Some of them did with surprising alacrity, but they themselves were usually caught quickly because they offered so much surface at which to grab.

In the meantime the older men would have been playing dominoes in the small back room. Forty-two was the game of dominoes which the church goers used as a substitute for card games. It was a game with drawn hands and bids, somewhat like the game of Five Hundred with cards and a very good game.

At smaller parties in private houses or in the smaller room in the firehouse, quieter kissing games were played. Catch would have been destructive to any parlor. It could have been played in the firehouse, but the building was getting old and the floor support deemed too feeble for such violence. For these post office was the standard game. A corner closed off with screens or an adjoining hall was selected as the post office, a post master or mistress appointed to guard the door, and then a boy or girl retired into the post office and sent out word that there were so many letters for so-and-so. Each letter meant a kiss, and the length of time of delivery could be stretched out until either the recipient or the chaperone of the party protested. Forfeits was another common game in which the forfeit might be to kiss somebody, usually the wrong person, or to do some silly and laughable act either alone or with a partner.

Other small party games were spin-the-platter, musical chairs, and occasionally though not often, charades.

These were the accepted forms of evening entertainment in the community. They satisfied us younger ones who knew nothing better. A few thought catch too strenuous and unladylike, and a few thought all of the kissing games unsanitary. There was one girl who would let herself be kissed only on the back of her hand. And there were a few others who thought all the kissing games boring and stayed home and read.

For those in the village and the countryside who were already on the road to hell there were two saloons, one in each of the old hotels, and a pool room in each. Here the lost souls congregated, and against them the righteous fulminated. The saloon of the Chapman House particularly incurred wrath, because being in the very middle of the village it set a bad example to any youth who passed by it. I was warned when I went to the village never to go into the Chapman House. When I walked past, I could always smell the odor of beer from the saloon door, and if it was late in the day old Doc Marsh would be sitting on the veranda, tipped back in his chair, feet in the air, head against the wall, dead drunk and snoring.

He epitomized for me the mysterious terror of the saloon. He was certainly an example of the degredation to which drink could bring an intelligent man. He had once been a practicing doctor in the village. I never heard the cause of his descent to alcohol. He lived in one of the good houses of the area, the only family house built of stone, but built evidently in Victorian years, for its architecture was Gothic. There were two sisters and Doc, all unmarried. Though his sisters kept a good home for him, he had become a daily fixture of the Chapman House. He was sad to contemplate, but harmless enough.

Along with its disreputable saloon and pool room, the Chapman House still had one remnant of former grandeur, its ballroom. It was a long hall on the second floor of the building, an extension really, projecting over the stables and the carriage room. The entrance was by a narrow wooden stairway next to the covered driveway by which teams entered the rear of the hotel. Like the second story of the Red Men's Hall, it was a perfect fire trap, but nobody thought about fire traps in those days, witness the many two- and three-story wooden hotels at vacation resorts all over the eastern United States.

The ballroom was now the meeting place of the GAR, the Grand Army of the Republic, the Civil War's edition in the North of the American Legion. The GAR men, whose standards of behavior had been somewhat liberalized by the war, not only had no objection to dancing but gave annual blowouts called bean bakes, which were essentially dances. The bean bakes were held in mid-winter, when the sleighing was good. The news of one to come was spread far and wide, to Braman's Corners and Ryder's Corners and Charleston Four Corners, to Schoharie and Middleburg and Polly Hollow (pronounced holler), even to Altamont and Amsterdam.

For the event the GAR spent time and money liberally. They imported an orchestra all the way from Fort Plain up the Mohawk Valley. They decorated the ballroom with streamers of red, white, and blue crepe paper. They set up long stretcher tables on the dance floor. And on the day they set the two stoves going until they were red hot at their bellies.

Old Bill Tulloch always helped with this. He was even a more permanent fixture of the Chapman House than Doc Marsh. He was in his seventies and had no family, no home. Sometimes one or another village family befriended him a while, but most of the time he hung around the Chapman House as a choreboy. When he was sober he carried water for the kitchen, tended the stoves, and kept the stables clean. When he was drunk he slept in one of the stalls on a pile of hay.

The orchestra for the bean bake arrived late in the afternoon, drums and fiddles and men in a big sleigh behind a team of horses. Old Bill took care of the horses while the orchestra men carried their instruments up into the ballroom and came back down to the saloon. Doc Marsh, anticipating the excitement, had already drunk himself asleep in one corner. In the kitchen Mrs. Chapman was heating rum on the cook stove.

By five o'clock those of the village folk who dared to be seen in the Chapman House began to arrive, carrying under their arms dishes of warm baked beans or scalloped potatoes. Then from the hills the farmers came on bobsleighs or in cutters, and from the neighboring villages came big sleighs cushioned with straw, among which human beings lay packed like breakable pottery in excelsior.

The meal came first, served on the stretcher tables in the ballroom. After the meal there had to be a political speaker, since it was a GAR party. But the evening really began when the tables had been removed from the stretchers and set against the wall, the drums set up beside the old square piano, the fiddler scraped over his strings and worked them into tune, and the caller shouted, "Fill up the floor!"

Whatever joy and strength and beauty molded the flesh and the mind of the hill farmer came out transformed in his square dancing. It was one stream of artistic expression that flowed undammed. The sunlight on April slopes, the swing of the crow flocks over their roosting pines, the shower winds of midsummer that lifted haycocks over the treetops, the red maples in October, the blast of the north wind in January, all these molded him, and all of these moved in his square dancing. Leather-faced farmers with calloused hands and knotted fingers could sashay like a young maple swaying in the wind. Huge-boned farm women with two hundred pounds of flesh could swing with the smoothness of water flowing over polished boulders.

It was an art in which they took pride. To miss a step, to

make a mistake in a set, was unpardonable. Any square dancer was supposed to know intimately all the movements of the many dances that might be called during the evening. To know how to swing a partner properly was as important as knowing the multiplication tables. From the simple elementals of "right and left six" and "all gents to the right," up through "duck and dive six" and "birdie fly out and crow fly in," to that most complicated of all square dances, the Fireman's Dance, it was essential to know not only where one should be at each moment of the dance and what one's hands and feet should be doing at the moment, but also that they should be doing each movement in time to the music.

The jigs that ended each set were always the most hilarious. They were the dances in which most of the swinging was concentrated. It was always a trick of the men to try to swing the women off their feet, and the trick of the women to keep their toes touching the floor at the proper beats and never let themselves be lifted in the air like sacks of grain. During the jigs often came "make a basket," the roughest of all square dance movements, when each set of eight persons with arms interlocked swung around in its circle like a top. It was a test of arm muscle and of clothes. The women came out of it flushed and giggling, adjusting their dresses into place while they went into "allemande left."

In the full of the evening, when the ballroom was resounding with voices and laughter like waves beating in a sea cave, the orchestra would play *Chicken Reel* for a jig. Long before jazz orchestras were thought of, it utilized the modern idea of a single player "getting hot," playing an improvised solo while the rest of the players either kept quiet or drummed time. *Chicken Reel* always made the old men slap their feet to the floor and stop on their way around the set to do a few steps of a solo jig.

In those days orchestras did not play by union rules. A

dance ended when there was nobody left to dance, and that might easily be two, three, or even four o'clock in the morning. These later quieter hours, when eyes were getting heavy, was the time for that square dance movement whose music is the loveliest of all square dance music, "sashay by your partner," the love song of the square dances, nearest in grace to the minuet of the German dances.

At last everybody was worn out. Mrs. Chapman's hot rum was nearly gone, and the orchestra men put their instruments in their cases and came downstairs. Old Bill Tulloch, half drunk, staggered out to harness their team to the sleigh. Mrs. Chapman fortified the men for their long ride with a last drink of hot rum, and they drove off in the white starlit night up the village street for the hills to the north, the sleigh bells jingling.

The bean bakes were at their height of popularity at about the turn of the century. But their popularity dwindled as the popularity of the kissing games increased. By 1910 most of the old men left in the GAR were too feeble to dance. Their bean bakes disappeared, dances were infrequent. This was the time when revival meetings were becoming more and more popular in the churches. Scarcely a winter passed in which one of the churches did not have a week of revival services, with an imported minister thundering the terrors of hell. I never attended one, for my father disapproved of revival meetings and would neither go himself nor let me go. "They only terrify the children," he said. "It's a shame." But the power of the church disciplines was more and more in evidence in the community. By now the ones who dared to dance did not represent more than ten percent of the countryside, if that.

They were a small and ignored group. But they were important, for out of them, not out of the kissing game crowd, was to come the popular entertainment of almost half of the century and the germ of much of its popular music.

I have tried to figure, without much success, the cause of the intellectual stagnation of Esperance during the last quarter of the nineteenth century. Why did a village that had prided itself on being the intellectual center of the county come to be merely a collection of shopkeepers and retired farmers, whose outlook went little beyond the events of daily living? Where did the intellectual curiosity go?

Perhaps it was because Esperance did not grow while other towns in the county, Schoharie, Cobleskill, and Middleburg, did grow. Or perhaps the coming of the railroad to replace the stagecoaches on the turnpike had begun to pull its young to the industrial centers, as the automobile was later to do so much more effectively. Perhaps it was mere chance. Whatever the reason, by the turn of the century, most of the intellectual elite of Esperance were gone. Ed Clark, who published the only newspaper the village ever boasted, went in search of a milder climate first to Chattanooga, Tennessee, and later to Tucson, Arizona. Harry Hazelton, whose father had been in the consular service at Genoa, Italy, went to New York city to become a newspaper man. The Seeley family, two spinster school teachers and a bachelor brother, left for the Bronx, which was then a prosperous section of New York City. Al Swan, the stonecutter from Scotland, moved to Schoharie. Mr. Bissell, for years the village school teacher and an exceedingly intelligent man, left for Seattle.

For the few that were left, the prospect of the meeting of active mind with active mind was meager. In the time of my childhood, the best example was Dr. Paul Moore, probably the most intelligent man of the countryside. Dr. Paul Moore never went to the church socials and played kissing games. To a man of his mind, kissing games must have seemed infantile amusement.

His family was the last remnant of the cultural Esperance of the 1800s. Paul must have been a brilliant youth. He had gone to Albany Medical College, spent a year in Germany studying, and then come back to Esperance to practice. He was a middle-aged man when I first remember him, tall, thin, with a face resembling pictures of Emerson. He lived in a small house on the Back Street with two sisters. The young sister, Louise, had been unhappily married, and after the death of her husband had in the Victorian way retired to her couch as an invalid. Neither the older sister, Abbie, nor Doctor Paul had ever married. Abbie, a short thin active woman with a wiry voice, cared for the three of them.

In their younger days the house had been a center for social gatherings, evenings of singing songs around the parlor organ, eating popcorn, and talking. By now each of the three had retired inwardly. Doctor Paul, perhaps for lack of minds in the village equal to his own, found the satisfaction of his flesh in several of the more careless married or unmarried women of the countryside, and the satisfaction of his mind in reading. He had a small but good library, Thoreau, Emerson, Longfellow, Goethe, Whittier, and the best of the English essayists.

His office was a tiny room at the back of the house. It contained one glass secretary for a desk, the shelves full of books, a row of shelves across from the secretary full of bottles of pills and medical materials, one chair for the doctor and one tiny straight chair for the patient, and at the end of the office behind a green curtain the Doctor's narrow bed.

In a small barn behind the house he kept a horse, a gig, a carriage, and a cutter. In the summer he usually made his calls about the countryside in the gig, in the winter with the cutter. His charge for office calls was usually fifty cents, which included the medicine prescribed. For delivering a baby his charge was five dollars. The delivery was done in the home, without midwife or nurse, though sometimes a neighbor came in to help with the housework until the mother could get out of bed and do it herself.

It must have been a lonely life he led in Esperance without matching minds to hold his interest and without entertainment but what he made for himself. There were, however, certain common diversions that anybody could enjoy, boating on the crick, fishing, skating in the winter. I cannot remember that Doctor Paul ever went skating, though he may have done so in his earlier days. But he did like to fish, and the hour he spent on the crick in a boat, or the hours spent driving his one-horse gig over the country roads to a patient must have been his recreation hours, when his mind puzzled the enigmas of life while his eyes enjoyed the scenes about him, those, and the hours at night in his office reading a book.

Most of the people of the village, young and old, men and women, liked to fish. The game fish of the crick was the small-mouth black bass, and it was such a good game fish that its presence brought many summer boarders to the village. It is a fish of swift water or deep water. Above the dam, where the water was quiet, a bass might occasionally be caught from shore, but for the big ones a boat was needed to get out into the deep water. Below the dam one fished for bass by wading into the swift water and letting the line float out to just where the foaming light green water began to merge into the quieter green depths.

The best bait for bass was the larvae of the dobson fly. These were to be found under the stones in the rifts. Expert fishermen got their dobson by wading in the rifts with a wire screen, turning over the big stones, and collecting the dobson as they were washed onto the screen. They were then stored in a can fastened to the belt. But young boys made a little money by hunting dobson and selling them. The boys' method was to work without a screen, turn over a stone and grab the dobson quickly before it was washed away, and then store it temporarily not in a can at the belt but in the hair of the head under the tight caps that were then the universal headdress for men. It was common for a boy to have half a dozen live dobson an inch or two long crawling about in his hair under his cap. Though they could pinch viciously, they never seemed to do so when they were in one's hair.

Many families of the village had their own flat-bottomed rowboat kept chained to a tree or post along the banks of the crick in summer, and drawn high out of the water's reach and inverted for the winter. The best time for boating or fishing from a boat was late in the afternoon. Many families used to take a picnic lunch and row up the crick to a small side brook called the Cove, or farther on up to Cold Springs, where a gush of cold water came out through a hole in the yellow clay of the crick bank. They would fish a little on the way up, disembark and eat their supper under elms in the late afternoon on the bank of the crick, and then drift slowly back down to the village after supper, fishing on the way in the hour just before dusk when bass were apt to be biting best. For fishing in the deep water, minnows were used as well as dobson, and occasionally crickets, which were not so good. Some of the summer boarders, however, often brought commercial fly hooks and spun their silk lines out over the water at this hour.

Those who had no boat sat on the banks and fished with long bamboo poles baited with fishworms for sunfish and rock bass or whitefish, all good eating.

In the winter everybody skated, young and old. Once the crick had frozen solid, one could skate all the way to Sloansville, four miles, and back. In the evenings there was usually a fire built on the ice at the end of Crick Street. If there was snow on the ice, the boys would clear off a large area, around which couples or single persons could skate, coming now and then to the fire to warm cold fingers.

Bobsledding, more daring and dangerous, attracted a few of the old, but mostly the young. In the days before autos and snow plowing, a group could drag a bobsled to the top of the hills on the way to Oak Nose and then go careening down the packed snow of the road at a tremendous speed. It was an exciting sport. The dangers were making the curves of the road successfully or meeting a team of horses on the road and having to swerve off the road into a snowbank when going full speed. Much depended upon the skill of the man steering the bobsled, but there were often tumbles and occasionally serious injuries.

Walking as a recreation was little indulged, except at two times of year, in the early spring when women and children went to the woodlots to pick mayflowers, and in autumn when even men went nutting. In the early days there were chestnuts, the sweetest nut of the countryside, but after the destruction of the chestnut trees by blight, there still remained the nuts of the shagbark hickory. For these one went to the known groves with a sack over his shoulder just after the first frost, when the nuts were falling from the trees and before the squirrels had time to collect them all.

None of the farmers had much time for any of these diversions, except perhaps getting their winter supply of hickory nuts from their own trees. Nor did they have energy left for them after the long days of farm work. Their usual evening diversion was to read the daily paper or the *Farmers' Almanac* until their eyes drooped and then go to bed.

My father was always in bed by nine o'clock at night. He never, in my memory, had any inclination toward sports. Things of the mind, ideas, interested him, and like Doctor Paul Moore, he suffered, I am sure, from the want of intellectual stimulus. He never let the life of a farmer dull his mind. He read magazines and books, he followed the course of national events with critical analysis, and like most country folk, he loved to argue about almost anything. Not long after he bought Oak Nose, he also bought one of the old Oliver typewriters, with a touch hard enough to wear out a lady's hand, and with this he began to record random ideas, and even went to the extent of

writing two or three short stories. Unfortunately, having written them, he had no idea of what to do with them except to
show them to his friends, who read them with polite disinterest,
and to my mother, whose reading was limited to the Sunday
school quarterlies, and whose disinterest was scarcely polite.

Had he been surrounded with friends whose minds
were as sharp and as world curious as his own, he might have
been prodded into becoming a writer. His mind had always had
a philosophical bent, and as the years went on his obsession
with philosophy increased, and he tried to write out his own
philosophical scheme of the universe, but he worked against
lack of knowledge. His early training had all been religious. He
had gone to school at Poultney, Vermont, a Methodist school,
and the Bible still remained the basic influence on his thinking.
He had no scientific training whatever, and though quite willing to accept Darwin's theory of evolution, he never really
brought himself to face the adjustments it set for any
philosophical scheme of the universe. Had he been among a
group of friends with varied intellectual interests, he might
have been forced to question more deeply some of his funda-
mental beliefs. But it takes a mind of genius to break through
alone the chains of its generation. My father, like Doctor Paul
Moore, went his way alone.

Coming and Going

All of my childhood we had never had a buggy. In the summer we had three ways of going to the village, the democrat wagon, the lumber wagon, and the buckboard. If it rained, we held an umbrella over our heads and let our feet get wet. The buckboard seat was so narrow that I usually rode on the flat wooden rear with my feet dangling off. Sometimes the village boys laughed at me for riding so. "Dangle-legs!" they taunted.

I wanted a buggy. I teased my father to get one.

"A buggy costs money," he said.

"How much money?" I asked.

"Oh, fifty, sixty, maybe seventy dollars."

That silenced me. I was old enough to know that we could never spend that much money at one time, except for the interest on the mortgage. But I still wanted a buggy. I pondered over the problem many days. Then the big idea came to me.

"Can't I take the money out of my bank and buy a buggy?"

My bank was one of the small iron savings banks with a slot in the side. I had had it ever since I could remember. I had put my pennies and nickels and dimes in it, and whenever it got full my father would unscrew its two halves, count the money, and replace it by bills, which he stored for me in a tin box in a bureau drawer. It was all saved until I was old enough to spend it on something worthwhile.

Now my father and mother were up against a problem. Was a buggy something worthwhile for a boy of nine to buy?

My mother got out my money and counted it. I had a little over fifty dollars.

"You said we could get a buggy for fifty dollars," I told my father.

"We'll see," my father said, and I gave up hope, for that was usually my father's gentle way of saying no.

Nevertheless, in a week or two a catalog arrived from a wagon manufacturing firm. Then in short time another came, and still another. They came addressed to me.

"Who knows I want a buggy?" I demanded.

"I do," my father said. "I sent for the catalogs."

We studied the catalogs together. But the buggies that could be bought for fifty dollars didn't look worth having.

"Well, if we found what we wanted," my father said, "and you didn't have money enough, maybe your mother and I could make up what you lacked."

I went at the catalogs with a zest. And I soon enough found what I wanted. It was a split hickory buggy. It was made somewhere in Indiana, and it cost sixty-five dollars. The moment I saw the picture of it I knew it was the one I wanted. It looked big. It had side curtains, it had a buggy lamp on its dash, and its seat was wide enough for all three of us.

My father liked it too. He and my mother talked it over a long time, and in the end they said we would buy it. My father cleaned all of the change out of my bank. He got the bills out of the tin box in the bureau drawer. He emptied his own pocketbook. My mother took her five-dollar bill out of the blue pitcher on the what-not. We went to the village in the buckboard, and my father sent a money order for the buggy.

It was nearly a month coming by freight. It came all crated up like a baby carriage. My father went to the depot with the team and the lumber wagon. The station master helped him load the crate on the back of the wagon, and we drove home with it. My mother stood in the driveway and watched us drive up to the barn.

I could hardly wait until we got the horses unhitched. I wanted to uncrate the buggy and put it together myself, but my father said, "Don't be in such a hurry. You don't want it to fall apart the first time we go to the village, do you?"

We slid it off the lumber wagon. Then my father began to uncrate it. He was slow and methodical. As he took off each board of the crate, he pulled all of the nails out of it before he laid it down and took off another. I fidgeted and poked and got in the way. But one by one the parts came out of the crate, the wheels, the top, the thills, and at last the box itself.

As soon as the wheels were on, I jumped inside and bounced up and down on the seat. The upholstery was green worsted, warm to the touch. The fresh leather of the dashboard shone like a looking glass.

"I guess it's a nice one," my father said.

It was to me. It surpassed all my dreams. When it stood assembled, with its top and shining thills waiting, I said eagerly, "Are we going to try it out?"

"Now?" my father said laughing. "Just like your mother! Want to show everything off the minute you get it. Too late today. Tomorrow, maybe. We'll leave it sit here tonight."

All evening I was in and out of the buggy. I felt the wheels. I inspected the top. I put on the side curtains. I filled the carriage lamp and lit it. I put the best whip in the whip socket.

Next morning I was up early. "We can drive Nancy Hanks, can't we?" I asked my father, and he agreed. Nancy Hanks was our new horse. She was old, actually. My uncle, who ran a grocery store in Schenectady, had given her to my mother because she was too old to use any longer on the grocery delivery wagon. But she was a well-built mare, not a farm horse like Tom or Jack, and she still had spirit.

I shined Nancy Hanks as I had never shined her before. As soon as the chores were done we went to the village. My father let me sit behind the whip socket and drive. Nancy Hanks knew her rig. When I turned into the main street of Esperance, she picked up her heels and danced. I held tight on the lines and let her have her way. At the turn into the church shed I saw Minard Parker, the minister's son, playing with some other boys on the parsonage steps. They were the ones who had laughed at me for riding on the back of the buckboard. Nancy Hanks took the entrance to the shed at a trot. The fresh wheel rims ground over the sidewalk. I shoved both lines into one hand, like an old driver, and waved at the boys.

It remains even now the one triumphant entry of my life.

It is true that there was an anticlimax to the triumph. When I got in back of the church and tried to drive under the shed, I found that the top of the buggy was so high that it would not go under the beam. So we had to get out and put the top down before we could drive to a stall. And always afterwards, even if it was pouring rain, we would have to put the top down to drive under the church shed. Once when my mother was driving she forgot, and got the buggy stuck just under the eaves of the shed. Luckily the minister discovered her predicament and helped her extricate the buggy without injury to the top.

For the first year I kept it always washed and spotless, but after that the novelty was gone. It became a part of our living. It carried us to the village to shop, to church, to picnics, to socials, to the depot to meet guests. The mud of the dirt road collected on its hubs and along the springs and axles. Once or twice a season I got around to washing it, but on a farm one has little time for washing wagons. It lasted well, all through my school days and until I had graduated from college. And it was sold, still good, when my father finally gave up keeping a horse. But by that time it was an obsolete method of transportation.

The Delaware and Hudson Railroad, on its route from Binghamton to Albany, crossed the Schoharie a few miles south of Esperance. The nearest it came to Esperance was halfway up the south valley side, and there, a mile and a half from the village, was the railroad station. There was some talk of another railroad going west from Albany that would enter the village. A survey was even made, but this was just after the crest of railroad development, and before the railroad could ever be begun, the machine had appeared that was to supersede it, the machine that was more than any other mechanical invention to change completely the whole village of Esperance and the lives of the people in it.

The farmers of the valley first thought of the automobile as a curse. When they went to the village it terrified their horses and sent them into the ditches, overturning the light buckboards. Even the oldest plug would rise on his heels in the thills and snap the traces. Women no longer dared to drive. Anywhere along the road an automobile might come charging up in a cloud of dust or under a funnel of steam.

As a matter of fact, the drivers of the first automobiles feared a horse and buggy as much as the horses feared the automobile. No one knew what a horse might do, and if it ran away and broke the wagon or injured the driver, a jury might judge the driver of the automobile responsible for the damage.

The first two automobiles in Esperance were owned by the two village sports, John VanVechten, president of the insurance company, and my uncle; Barlow Vunck, the hay dealer. John VanVechten bought the first one, a red Maxwell. It was open to the wind and rain. It had two seats, the second built high in the back and called a tonneau (pronounced in the village *ton-u-wah*) seat. When my Uncle Barlow saw John VanVechten go down Main Street in the red Maxwell, he promtly went to Albany and bought a Jackson, a huge lumbering tub with two seats on the same level, a top, no doors, and two huge shifting levers that stuck up on the outside next to the driver's seat. Then the race was on.

It was not a race of cars, for they were both too polite and not sufficiently friendly with each other for that. Each tried to show his machine off to the most townsfolk in the most appealing way. They drove up and down Main Street. They filled the high seats with guests in linen dusters and went for rides in the country and got stuck in mudholes. The Jackson had a bad water cooling system and was always boiling its radiator and shooting volcanoes of steam up in front. The Maxwell had no power and was always getting stuck on steep hills.

When either car went up the street there was always a crowd of kids running after it, and at the sound of its chugging past, all the women of the houses rushed to their front windows and pulled aside the lace curtains and stared.

Sunday mornings, while their wives went to church, John VanVechten in his barn and my Uncle Barlow in his barn cleaned their prizes with soap and water and chamois and dust cloth. They shined the brass to a mirror surface. They wiped every grain of dust from the leather seats. No thoroughbred horse was ever better groomed. But they never went riding in their autos on Sundays. That would have been defying too dangerously the moral standards of the villagers, upon whom their patronage depended.

I well remember my first ride. It was Fourth of July.

There was an ice cream and strawberry festival on the Methodist church lawn, and I was standing in front of the church with a bunch of kids. My Uncle Barlow drove up in front of the church with my mother and three or four girl cousins in the Jackson. I offered a fine excuse for stopping the automobile in front of the crowd. My cousins called to me and I ran out and climbed into the back seat and pushed down into the few inches of seat space left for me. I cannot remember much about the actual ride. I remember the getting in and the coming back. My Uncle Barlow stopped again in front of the group of ice cream eaters to let me out. I sauntered back across the lawn, trying to be nonchalant, as if a ride in an automobile were something that happened every day in my life. The boys all crowded around me. "What was it like? Is it fun? Did you get stuck?"

I shrugged my shoulders. "Not much different than being in a buckboard behind a horse."

John VanVechten began to fear that the Maxwell was not as impressive as my Uncle Barlow's Jackson. After much consideration, he bought a White Steamer. It burned charcoal, and long before one went for a ride he had to go out in the barn and fire it up. But it was black and luxurious looking. It had a top and a windshield and doors on the front seat.

The steamer made my Uncle Barlow take stock. However, he still had one up on John VanVechten. His daughter, Gertrude, had learned to drive the Jackson. It is true that she had knocked out the side of old Jerry's stall the first time she drove into the barn. Nevertheless she persisted. She drove around the village's one block and scared one horse into a runaway. She drove to Sloansville and back, four miles away. She even learned to change a tire. And none of the women of John VanVechten's family had yet learned to drive.

But my Uncle Barlow was still not satisfied. The Jackson was beginning to look old fashioned. Since its time front doors and windshields had appeared. At first my Uncle

Barlow had scoffed, "I'll never have a windshield on my car and get knocked through a pane of glass." But there was John VanVechten with his new steamer, with windshield and front doors. My Uncle Barlow went to Albany with the Jackson, thirty miles, an all-day trip. When he came back the Jackson had a windshield and doors. The Jackson firm had already anticipated his desires and was supplying fixtures to be added to their first cars.

All the roads about the village were full of hazards for automobiles. The only one at all level was the four-mile stretch along the Schoharie to Sloansville, but this advantage was offset by its clay base. If a thundershower came up while an automobile was on the road, the chances were that the automobile either slid into a ditch or got stuck in a mudhole and from either disaster was rescued only by the nearest team of horses. On the road to Burtonsville, along the Schoharie in the other direction, there were two steep gullies that made drivers hold the steering wheel tight going down and everybody lean forward in their seats on the way up, praying for power to reach the top.

All the other roads were hill roads. For an automobile the curse of these was the thank-you-ma'ams, those ridges built across the grades to divert water to the ditches. They were nice places for a tired horse to rest, but on an automobile they produced an earthquake shock. Some of them were so high, and the ditch on the upper side so deep, that an automobile going up would lodge its front wheels in the ditch, its back wheels on the lower foothills of the ridge, and its underparts firmly grounded on the peak. For such mishaps there was always the same recourse, the nearest farmer and his team.

The third man in the village to be bitten by the auto bug was Doctor Norwood. Doctor Norwood was in his sixties, but he still had sporting ideas. The car he bought was a Brush. It was small and red as a fire truck. It had two cylinders and a

Cousin Gertrude Vunck, seated in buggy, was the first woman in Esperance to drive an automobile. Old Dan, here hitched up and in his prime, lived his later years at Oak Nose Farm. He was a gift from Uncle Barlow Vunck, who owned one of the village's first autos.

chain drive. When it came down the street it sounded like a distant locomotive chugging up a steep grade. When it came close the rasping gr-gr-gr-gr of the chain drive sounded as if something inside were being ripped apart.

The company salesman brought the car to the village and took the doctor out for a driving lesson. The doctor got along very well with the salesman beside him. He was very pleased with his purchase. He left it standing in the driveway beside his house, and the salesman left town. Later in the day the doctor went out and took another drive by himself. When he came back home, he decided to put the machine into the barn. The barn stood a little downhill at the end of the driveway beside the house. The Brush putted and ground its way down the driveway faster than the doctor had anticipated. He lost his head and hit the side of the barn door instead of the open space.

Nothing was damaged much except the doctor's self-confidence. That suffered from the same terror that struck all the horses. He got somebody to drive the Brush into the barn for him, and there it stayed. After a week or two the doctor got courage enough to go to the barn, jack up the rear wheels of the Brush, start the engine, get into the seat, and work the gear shift. That was a second beginning. He thought he might learn to drive that way. For a long time he used to go into the barn and sit in the little one-seated Brush, with the motor putt-putting and the chain grinding its gr-gr-gr-gr under him, and he shifting the gears with infinite care. But that was as far as he ever got. Never again could he screw up his courage to the point of letting the rear wheels off the jacks before he got into the driver's seat. Now and then he hired someone to let it down and take him for a drive, but not often. His pride was hurt, the satisfaction gone. When he died, some years later, the little red Brush, already an antique, still stood in his barn on the jacks, and was sold at his auction.

In the meantime John VanVechten had advanced to one of the new air-cooled Franklins, and my Uncle Barlow to a Cadillac. But also in the meantime came a momentous step. The first hard-surfaced road near the village was constructed, the mile-and-a-half stretch between the village and the railroad station.

For us local boys the building of the road was the most exciting thing that had ever happened. A big steam engine and roller, which we had never seen before, moved in. A machine for crushing stone was set up. Then came a few Italian laborers, for the big immigration into the United States at that time was from Italy. We called the workers Wops. We found them romantic, being the first foreigners we had ever met. They told us stories about Italy in broken English, and they taught us to swear in Italian before some of us knew completely what we were saying.

The mile-and-a-half stretch of road took about a year to build and gave immediate impulse to the purchase of automobiles in the village. It became the boulevard up and down which the automobiles paraded, with their sides streaming with the wind-flapped veils of the women. But it was hard on one person, old Richard Hunter, who drove the "express" to carry passengers and freight from the railroad station to the village. His vehicle was in summer a two-seated surrey pulled by a team, and in winter a two-seated sleigh. One might have expected him to buy an automobile, but no, he was too old to learn new tricks. He had driven horses all his life, and he would drive horses to the end, even though the new pavement was hard on the horses' hoofs and upon the iron rims of the surrey wheels, and often when there was room he drove along the side of the road to make the going easier and quieter.

In 1910 the first garage opened in the village. Before that everybody had repaired his own automobile. Now the garage, with a tank to supply gasoline, was the first rival to Frank Cornell's blacksmith shop.

If any single event can be marked as the turning point of Esperance in the twentieth century, the construction of the Esperance depot road was it, for the automobile was to shatter the isolation and self-sufficiency of the village, to transform the community from one of farmers to one of city commuters, of shop and office workers. It was to transform Main Street from a picturesque elm-lined vista to a wide plain of concrete cutting off the ends of all the lawns along the street. For the quiet, dusty afternoons of the horse-and-buggy days it would substitute the noise and the air pollution of automobile traffic. It would make the village for at least thirty years lose its identity and become merely another slow traffic nuisance on U.S. 20, the northern east-west highway across the United States. And the first definite mark of that transformation on the countryside was that mile and a half of narrow concrete road.

We Move to the Village

*D*uring the later years of my boyhood at Oak Nose my father was facing a problem. Each of the successive teachers at the Rock School had reported the pleasing but at the same time disquieting story: I, his child, deserved an education.

In the year 1910 the education of a farm child was not a simple thing. In Esperance not even a high school was available, only a two-room elementary school. The simplest way for me to attend high school was to commute by train fifteen miles twice a day. Oak Nose was three miles from the railroad station. I would be ready for high school at thirteen. A three-mile walk twice a day during our winter blizzard weather sounded dangerous. The other alternative was to send me to board in a town with a high school. But this would require money.

The mortgage was still on the farm. None of the principal had been paid. We had lived well in the eight years at Oak Nose, but my father had put no money in the bank. After the death of my grandfather, the wages of a hired man ate up the profits. Where was the money for my education to come from?

It was then that my mother began to say, "If we went to live in the village, Freddie would be able to walk the mile and a half to the depot."

"If we went to live in the village. . . ." The words must have sounded like a tolling death knell to my father. Not that life on the farm had been all happy. Certainly it had not been as he had dreamed it. He had not minded the hard work, but the household life had not gone smoothly. My mother was always complaining, first about the presence of Mahala, and after Mahala left, about the work the hired men made for her. She had never been able to become the farmer's wife my father had dreamed of.

Why had she been unable to adapt herself? I think it was primarily because the returns were so small. Coming from a thrifty German family with five children, raised in the village, she had come to measure things by dollars and cents. If one worked hard and got good money for it, that was all right, but to work hard, and then have to scramble for sixty dollars at the end of the year to pay the interest on the mortgage, that was disgusting. And there was also the galling fact that her brothers and sisters had done so much better by themselves. Only she had married a farmer, and we were not getting anywhere. We were the poor relations. Not all the independence of farm life could reconcile her to her lot.

Whether she seized upon the necessity of high school for me as a lever for her own desires, I never knew. If she did so, she probably never would have admitted it even to herself. But her remark about living in the village came more and more into the conversation.

"If we moved to the village. . . ."

If my father had been an inconsiderate man, he would have closed his ears. It was his misfortune to be an overly considerate man. I needed an education, and he would have to make it possible. Now thinking back, I realize with terrifying humility the disappointment he must have been facing in those years. He loved the farm and the animals on it. He had spent much hard work improving it. He had looked forward, I am sure, to my taking it over when he grew old.

He did not give up all at once. We would go live in the village for the four years of my high school time, and then we would come back to the farm. When my mother suggested that he go back to his trade of watch repairing, he would have none of it. He took a job as a helper in one of the village grist mills. Early in the spring of my last year in grade school, we packed our household things and moved into a rented house in town. Tom and Jack and some of the farm machinery were sold at auction. The farm was let out to a tenant farmer. Nancy Hanks and the split hickory buggy went with us to the village.

I adapted myself quickly to village life. I learned to fish, to swim, to plague Frank Cornell, and to masturbate. Masterbation would have come anyway, since I was at puberty, but with the village boys playing together in groups, forbidden vices spread quicker. I had never before lived near enough to the crick to enjoy it, and now it became almost a passion with me. Daily that first summer I roamed its sides, fishing with a bamboo pole or swimming at the swimming hole. The water itself fascinated me, the remains of the old mill dam, where black snakes slithered among the torn planks, the swift rifts beyond the dam where the black bass were, the smooth water above, where eel grass grew along the banks and sunfish waited at the edge of the eel grass.

I remember well the first time I went fishing. It was still spring, the water not yet low enough for the fish to be biting well. I dug fishworms and fished near the abutments of the bridge for two hours and caught only one little whitefish. But on my way home, walking over the edge of the crumbling dam, I saw a fish lying at the edge of a shallow pool among the boulders. It was dead, there was no doubt about that, but it still looked in good condition. I picked it up, handled it, threw it back, picked it up again, and carefully strung it by the gills over the piece of fishline tied to a stick on which I was carrying my one little whitefish. I took the two of them home. My mother cleaned them for me. We ate them for supper. Fortunately none of us got sick.

All the boys in the village learned to swim as soon as their mothers would let them go near the water. When we moved to the village, my mother made me promise that I would never go into the water unless an older boy who could swim was with me, for a boy had once drowned at the swimming hole. I promised glibly and broke my promise quickly. The swimming hole was near the end of Crick Street, where a huge elm leaning over the water had a rope tied to one of its more extended branches. Each spring it would be the adventure of one of the more daring boys to climb up into the tree and replace the old rope with a strong new one. One swung out on the rope and dropped into the water with a splash, or if one was more daring, turned himself in the air by a kick of the feet at just the proper moment before leaving the rope, and dove into the water. This took experience. A novice would usually land flat on the water and have the breath knocked out of him. Many of the village boys spent half their days at the swimming hole, swimming, lying in the sun, stealing corn from the nearest garden for a roast, or making cigarettes of cornsilk safe from the eyes of their parents.

Bathing suits were never thought of. They were used only by girls, who swam in more open places near the bridge and dam. But actually the girls did not swim much. Swimming seemed to be a boy's prerogative. The swimming hole was held to be sacred to boys swimming nude, and anyone who presumed to interfere with their pleasure was trespassing. If a boat with women in it went past, the boys simply sank in the deep water up to their necks and stayed there until the boat had passed on out of sight.

Though in 1912 an Indian had probably not been seen in Esperance for a hundred years, playing Indians was still one of our amusements. The banks of the crick, heavily overgrown with willows and weeds, offered hidden alleys in which to lurk and spy. Also they offered weapons. Along the damp banks of the entering brooks, the rank angelica grew in thickets, lacy in summer with fern-like leaves, but quickly browning and drying out to leave the head-high center stalk, hollow but firm, like a piece of light bamboo. These made perfect spears, and armed with them a group of us would sneak over a bank and descend with a whoop upon another unsuspecting group of boys. I suppose it was sheer luck that nobody lost an eye.

The covered bridge over the crick was as much a part of the life of Esperance as the crick itself. Because of the small settlement on the east side there was always considerable foot traffic across the bridge. There were no footpaths. The sides of the bridge were closed for a distance of eight feet up from the floor, with only a four-foot opening under the eaves to admit light. It was therefore dark, and it was long, three spans. A foot passenger was always in danger of being run down by a team of horses, or later by an automobile. To make sure of being safe, one either shrank against the nearest beam, or stepped up on one of the slanting beams and clung against the outer wall.

Over the entrance was the usual sign: ten dollar fine for any person driving his horse or team faster than a walk over this bridge. Under it one walked into semidarkness. Women hated the bridge. They were afraid to cross it alone, particularly at night. We boys loved it. We would climb up among the beams, and there hidden in the semidarkness leaning against the side walls pasted with advertisements of Kendall's Spavin Cure or Red Horse Plug, we would tell dirty stories and smoke cornsilk cigarettes.

But many adults too enjoyed the bridge. On hot summer days it was a cool and pleasant spot. One could walk out to the middle and step up on the **V** formed by the joining of two side timbers and stand with his head rising into the eave's gap to look out on the swallows skimming over the water below and to watch the people in rowboats fishing for bass in the quiet water upstream above the mill dam. A breeze usually blew through those upper spaces, and there came from below the half pleasant, half acrid smell of carriage dust and horse manure.

At one time of year it was a meeting place for everybody. This was when the ice went out in the spring. Though the mill dam was decaying, it still retained a quiet reach of water for several miles upstream, and there the ice froze thick in winter. When the spring thaws lifted the ice above the top of the dam, it broke into great cakes, sometimes the whole width of the crick, and spilled over the dam and came tearing down the muddy raging water against the abutments of the bridge. The bridge would shake and shiver with the smash of the big cakes. So at the first call of "The ice is going out!", half of the townsfolk would leave their work and run down the street and stand on the banks near the bridge. The daring ones would go out on the bridge and climb up on the beams and stand with their heads out of the eaves opening, watching the cakes pass underneath and feeling the bridge tremble.

In 1912 the bridge was exactly one hundred years old. The official beginning of the Cherry Valley Turnpike was an act of the New York State Legislature in 1792. In 1793 the first bridge was built across the Schoharie. Esperance did not exist then. The first bridge did not exist long either. Early and late, engineers have been deceived by the Schoharie, a pleasant dawdling stream in dry summer weather, a fierce river in spring and fall floods. The spring flood of 1799 swept away the new bridge. Thereupon the legislature, on March 15, 1799, passed an act which provided for the establishment of a Turnpike Corporation for the building of a new bridge.

Part of the funds of the Turnpike Corporation were

raised by a state lottery. Tickets were $5.00 each. A temporary uncovered bridge was built in 1799 which lasted for several years. Then in 1809 the contract for a new permanent bridge was given to Theodore Burr, a cousin of Aaron Burr, the same man who built the old covered bridge across the Mohawk in Schenectady. Burr completed the piers of the bridge and then mysteriously disappeared for two years. Eccentricity ran in the Burr family. In 1811 he returned and completed the bridge. It was opened to traffic in 1812, when Judge Olney Briggs paid $2.00 to drive the first team over the bridge.

It was a toll bridge. Part of one toll schedule reads: "For every sulky, chair or chaise with one horse, 12 cents; for every chariot, coach, or phaeton, 25 cents; for every score of hogs, 5 cents; for every cart or sled drawn by two oxen or horses, 6 cents." It was a prosperous venture. The Cherry Valley Turnpike, in those days before the Erie Canal, was an important commercial highway. Sometimes several hundred teams passed over the bridge in a day, and the monthly tolls were around one thousand dollars.

In 1862 the bridge was condemned as unsafe. Nobody later seemed to know why. Perhaps the state engineers merely thought the bridge was old enough. Perhaps a contractor anxious for a job did some lobbying. At any rate, no new bridge was built. The Civil War was on, money was scarce. The condemnation was forgotten, and traffic continued as ever. In 1887 the bridge was purchased jointly by the towns of Esperance and Duanesburg and made a free bridge. The passing of the toll was celebrated with ceremonies and a brass band.

In my first year in the village, Mag Brunk, the last toll gatekeeper, was still alive. I suppose Mag Brunk's name was Margaret, but I never heard her called anything but Mag. She lived in the old gatekeeper's house. The floor of the stoop of the house was just level with the sidewalk at the Esperance entrance to the bridge, and the rest of the house descended down the crick bank. Mag used to sit on the stoop keeping mental if no longer financial track of the rigs that went in and out of the bridge. She liked her beer and her cornncob pipe, and I think the vagaries of humanity must have amused her, for I remember her always sitting on the stoop with her feet up on the railing, chuckling to herself, the corncob pipe jutting from the corner of her shrunken mouth.

Not far up the street Frank Cornell, the morose blacksmith, did not look with such amusement on human nature. He was one of those persons that children quickly discover they can tease, and the village boys often made his life miserable. His shop was down in an alley by the crick. In winter the boys threw sticks at his closed door and then ran. The sticks did no harm, but they annoyed Frank. The first time that spring that I was with a bunch of boys who did it, I didn't know enough to run. They threw the sticks, and I stood puzzled in the middle of the alley. Frank, his face red with fury, rolled open the shop door and looked out. He had a hammer in his hand. I thought he was going to throw it at me. But he only growled contemptuously, "You better run back up the hills before you get hurt!" Then muttering to himself he rolled the door back shut.

By the end of our first summer in the village, my father had come to a half-hearted acceptance of his life as a miller's helper. My mother was happy that money was coming in regularly. And I was starting high school at Altamont fifteen miles east. I was not alone. At least twenty of us took the daily train to Altamont, and an equal number to Cobleskill, the same distance west. We were an exasperating nuisance to conductors and passengers, running up and down the aisles of the coaches, screaming and fighting.

Emma Lape glad to be back in the village, c. 1915.

It was the year 1913, the year that the Western world was to awake from its blind dream into a century of grim reality. Like most of my elders, I was blissfully ignorant of disaster. I was more worried that my mother and father would discover that I was daily stealing five cents from the family pocketbook in the little drawer of the bureau of their bedroom. I spent the five cents each noon for an ice cream soda at Mrs. Bray's drugstore on the corner across from the railroad station in Altamont.

Each day my mother packed me a good lunch, which I ate with the other commuting boys in the locker room of the high school, but I could not resist Mrs. Bray's ice cream sodas. They were one of the new delights that high school was teaching me, for the only ice cream sodas in Cromwell's ice cream parlor in Esperance were made by adding a scoop of ice cream to a bottle of Moxie or root beer in a glass, and they did not compete with the real thing that Mrs. Bray fizzed out of her nickel-plated soda faucet.

I liked high school. I was eager to learn. But I liked just as much the daily train ride, and even the mile-and-a-half walk to the Esperance depot. Several other boys and I were developing an interest in birds, and we spent our time along the road searching the branches for new migrants to add to our list. We were also good at keeping a sharp lookout for the express to the depot driven by old Richard Hunter, Poppy Dick as we called him. Poppy Dick was a little deaf, and we soon discovered that by waiting until his team and surrey had passed us, we could run after it and jump on the back and cling to the frame and ride a short distance before we were discovered and ordered off by a threatening flick of the whip from the dashboard.

The identifying of birds became more and more of an obsession all through my high school years. It took over my mania for fishing, which was wearing out. At first I had nothing for reference but a couple of articles in the *National Geographic* illustrated in color. Then a city aunt gave me a volume called *Birds of the World*. This had beautiful descriptions and illustrations of birds like the California condor and the stork and the bird of paradise, none of which I ever saw in the elms along the depot road. Eventually, I found in a neighbor's parlor one of the new two-volume sets of Eaton's *Birds of New York*, with its excellent plates by Louis Agassiz Fuertes. These became my mine of puzzlement and joy.

In high school I learned some of the laws of life in

biology and the joys of make-believe in Shakespeare's *As You Like It*. The autumn melancholy of Jacques was beyond me emotionally, but he was a new type of character. Living in the village, close to the characters that from Oak Nose I had seen only intermittently and briefly, I was awakening to humanity. I began to watch and to know people as individuals.

Esperance had its quota of oddities. Amie Clayton, the half-wit peddler and accordion player, though he did not live in Esperance, was as common a figure in the village as he had been on the farm roads. He was always present at outdoor festivals, picnics, ball games, playing his accordion and jigging for pennies.

The most extraordinary character in the village was Annie Denison. She lived with her mother, a small wizened woman with a sharp voice. Annie was in her forties, tall, sturdily built, with coarse hair, a heavy-skinned mannish face and a man's deep voice. Her eyesight was so bad that she had to wear glasses with bulging lens, which made her eyes look enormous, and even with these glasses she saw so badly that in church she had to hold the hymnal close to her face to read the words. She was reported to be a hermaphrodite. Her house was on the street that led to the swimming hole. In summer we boys passed it daily and shouted taunts at her, laughing when she roared back an answer. Once when she was sitting on the top step of the stoop with her skirts fairly high and her knees spread, I saw something that from a distance resembled a small boy's penis.

Being marked as a curiosity and teased had soured her disposition, whatever it may have been when she was young, and she was always ready to take offense at the slightest provo-cation, which children, often cruel, were always ready to give. She would howl curses at us on the street, or she would go to church and settle herself in a pew and suddenly be offended at something, or perhaps nothing, and jump to her feet and stomp out of the church, sometimes saying nothing, sometimes sobbing.

Our Fred Brown, with his huge stumbling flat feet, was just beginning to become a village character. He used to come often to our house and talk in the evenings with my father, for he was lonely for companionship. The Hammond typewriter was always getting out of order, and my father was the only one who could fix it for him. He still took the Hick's weather almanac, which he would bring for me to read and to look at the storm pictures. And he was beginning to become a weather prophet.

His father was dead. Fred lived with his mother, an anemic old lady with a high weak voice, and Tiny, his father's sister, a large elderly woman built somewhat like Fred, but taller. She was quite masculine and the dominant figure of the household. She had a way, when you visited them, of never talking at you but always over your head, and her eyes seemed constantly searching the corners of the room's ceiling, as if they saw somebody up there. The three of them lived in a small white house just across the crick from the village, and from there Fred tried to make a meager living by doing odd jobs in the village.

Undoubtedly the village character who influenced me most was Abbie McCarty, for it was she who developed my nascent love of flowers. Also I was thrown in almost daily contact with her, for my mother, now that she was in the village with free time on her hands, often went to visit Mrs. McCarty. Mrs. McCarty's two grandsons, Abbie's nephews, were also my closest school friends. And most of all, Abbie's father, Duke, had the biggest collection of Wild West and Daredevil Dick magazines in the village, which he kept in the loft over his harness shop, safe from the eyes of the women of the family. There we boys went to read them, though they never interested me much. I liked better the Horatio Alger books of the poor boys who always became rich, or the Rover Boys series, or the mawkishly sentimental love novels of Mrs. E.D.E.N. Southworth.

Abbie was now one of the new telephone operators. Esperance had had telephone service for only a couple of years. The house phones were the big wall phones with power generated by a crank. Some of the lines which ran out over the hills had as many as fifteen houses linked together, and listening for one's call was complicated. Our call in the last year at Oak Nose was four long and two short rings. The central office was a small switchboard in a little building next to the Chapman House. In a small town where everybody knew everybody else, the telephone operators were the town's phone book, long before telephone companies had thought of them. Calls were made by name, not by number. The operators knew not only the business facilities of the village but usually the whereabouts of the residents. It was common to call somebody and have the operator say, "Oh, he isn't home now. I just saw him go down the street." Or if one was going away for a few hours, he could leave word with the operator of his whereabouts and have his calls directed to the phone of a neighbor.

For years there was only one operator at the switchboard at a time, one from seven in the morning until two in the afternoon, and another from two until nine at night. There was not yet a night operator.

Abbie was the exasperating one of the operators. In the office she was slow and deliberate, and the more one whirled the crank to hurry her up, the slower Abbie would be in answering. When anybody had to wait a long time for the operator, he always said, "Well, Abbie must be on." Nevertheless, she was one of the kindest women in the village. She would do any legitimate favor that was asked of her, and she was already beginning to take care of her mother and father who were getting old.

Her hats were the curiosity and amusement of the village. They usually had bird wings or bunches of flowers or big bows on them, and she always wore them perched high on her head and tilted at the same slight angle. Besides her flowers and her family, the Methodist church was the center of her interest. She sang in the choir a strong and unmelodious soprano, and always sat in one of the front seats of the choir section, where her hats formed the focal point for that part of the church.

Her flower gardens were the most beautiful in the village. There were flowers everywhere inside and around the house. Along the walk leading in there were in early summer foxgloves and canterbury bells and madonna lilies, and later phlox and China asters, and in the late autumn fragrant stock. She raised all of her plants from seed. In spring the back kitchen, the back porch, and the space under a grape trellis were all full of little flat pans of seedlings. Once she saw I was interested, Abbie always tried to pass on her knowledge to me. "Now stock," she would say, "when you plant stock, you want to plant a lot of seed." She had a way of lingering over her consonants at the ends of words while her eyes stared fixedly at the plants or at me or at something in the distance. "A lot of them are always single, and you let them all begin to blossom and throw away the single ones before you put them in the garden."

Her nephews were a little afraid of her, for she could be sharp tempered when she was displeased. But since she liked my mother and never tried to exercise any parental discipline on me, we got along well.

She had studied elocution, a popular female acquisition of the day, and at village entertainments she was always ready to recite *Curfew Shall Not Ring Tonight* with a most dramatic rendition of the young girl swinging on the clapper of the church bell.

At the same time that I was learning how to cultivate

flowers from Abbie, I was learning music. The old family melodeon had burst its bellows, and my father had been induced by the village music teacher, who also sold second-hand pianos, to buy a piano for me. It was one of the early upright Estey pianos with a solid oak frame and an imported French action that had settled into a torpidity from which no reamings of felt bearings was ever able to redeem it, so that one could never do good trills on it. But it was basically an excellent piano with a solid base tone, and it held its tune well. Nellie Gordon had taught me the fundamentals of music, but now I had to convert the flaccid touch needed for the melodeon to the firm snap necessary to control the old Estey. Unfortunately, there was no good local piano teacher, and I had no good music. I came only upon a glimpse of things now and then from the pieces of good music that were sometimes printed in the *Etude* magazine along with skits for beginners called *Twinkle Toes*. My cousin Gertrude, she who had driven the open-seated Jackson, had a collection of the pieces of ragtime just appearing, such as *Hiawatha* and *Arrah Wannah*, as well as the banal compositions like *The Burning of Rome* so popular at the moment for parlor piano players. But my early sense of musical values was good, and the things that I played over and over again for my own enjoyment were those snatches from the *Etude*, the slow movement from Beethoven's *Pathetique*, Handel's *Where'er you Walk*, or some of the Chopin *Preludes*.

My interpretations must have been atrocious. I remember one evening when Dr. Paul Moore had come to visit my father, I sat down at the piano and launched into an *Etude* piano arrangement of Schubert's *Serenade*. Dr. Paul, who was just leaving, stood behind me until I had finished. Then he said with a chuckle, "Boy, that's not one of these latest one-steps you're playing. That's a love song. Go gently at it, boy, gently." Then he lifted his knee to the middle of my back and grabbing both shoulders, pulled them back. He always did this when he came to see us. "You don't want to get round-shouldered yet," he said.

He often came to visit my father, who though not highly educated was one of the best read men in the village. I was too young to appreciate Dr. Paul. I remember that he was taken by my interest in birds. "I've got a book down in my office you might enjoy," he said. "It's called *Walden*. It's by a New Englander named Thoreau. Come down some day and I'l let you borrow it."

I never went. I was too young to be bothered with anybody as old as Dr. Paul Moore. One always regrets later the friendships that discrepancy of ages blocks off.

As another outlet of my musical inclination I joined the village band. I had no instrument. The band leader lent me a tenor horn, which was almost half as tall as I was, and I learned the fingering of the valves and occasionally how to mouth a good tone. We rehearsed in the upstairs room of the old engine house, and we played for Memorial Day and Fourth of July parades, but I cannot remember that we ever gave a concert. My favorites were Sousa marches and that waltz composed by a band leader of an insignificant pueblo in Mexico, a band probably no better than ours, but a composition that went around the world, played by bands from Argentina to Ceylon, *Over the Waves*.

Music was coming also to the streets of Esperance, for phonographs were becoming better and louder. On a summer afternoon through the open windows of a house would come the sound of a tinny tenor singing, 'I want sy-UM-pathy, sy-UM-pathy" and a little farther down the street Dietta Ball's player piano rippling off *The International Rag*. Dietta's was the first and, as far as I know, the only player piano ever to be in the village. Dietta was not particularly musical, but the old parlor organ was becoming old fashioned and relegated either to the loft of the barn or the dump heap, and in its place the village housewife liked to have a piano, more as a piece of furniture than as a musical instrument. Dietta wanted a piano too, but she was a gay person and wanted her piano to be of some value. The player piano also had some sales value, for Dietta's mother-in-law, old Mrs. Ball, had taken it in her head to rival Cromwell's and had begun to sell ice cream (even more watered than Mrs. Cromwell's, the women said) in her parlor where the piano stood. Mrs. Cromwell met the new competition by adding a new flavor called "Italian Special" to her list.

Then there was the entertainment in the Red Men's Hall, to which Alice Moeller brought her phonograph and played records of Caruso and Tetrazzini.

Alice Moeller was one of the Gilchrist girls. They were the first to bring the more sophisticated atmosphere of New York to the village. Mr. Gilchrist, a thin short mild-mannered man, repaired shoes and sharpened lawnmowers. Mrs. Gilchrist was also thin and short, but she was as dominant as Mr. Gilchrist was self-effacing. She spoke with a low-pitched mannish voice and with a slight Brooklyn accent.

The daughters, Alice and Mary, had married in New York, spent the early years of their married life there, and then returned to Esperance, Mary with her husband and daughter, Alice with only her children, for Alice's husband still worked in New York and came up for visits and vacations. Both girls had inherited the aggressive personality of their mother, and rarely agreed with anybody, particularly with each other.

Mary's daughter, Ethel, was one of the most beautiful girls I have ever seen, and she was the pride of Mary's life. They returned to Esperance just at the time when the tango was beginning to sweep the world of dance. Ethel had taken tango lessons with a fine dancing teacher in New York, and Mary had pictures of her taken with the dancing teacher in fantastic back-bending poses. She made some effort to have Ethel teach us boys of the village to tango, but to our mothers at that time the tango was immoral, and we were quickly discouraged from having anything to do with such unseemly practices.

Mary was good looking and in manner hard as nails. She was the first woman I ever saw with rouge and lipstick. When she was angry she could swear with a vocabulary as ample as any man. She was good-hearted and lovable, but her temper was equal to that of her sister Alice, and to the continual amusement of the village and to their own continual unhappiness, they were always feuding violently. Over what they quarreled I don't remember. Perhaps each was jealous of the other. But at times they would walk past each other's house with their noses in the air and their eyes straight ahead. They were so full of anger that they would vituperate each other to anybody who would listen. There would be periods of reconciliation, and then they would start all over again.

I cannot say that Alice's effort to raise the cultural level of the village by playing Caruso and Tetrazzini was a success. The records were listened to quietly and were applauded. But the real reaction came out the next day when I heard my Aunt Mate discussing the evening with my mother.

"It sounded a little screechy to me," my Aunt Mate said, taking a deft stitch on the linen napkin which she had brought with her to embroider while she gossiped. "Anyway, I always thought a good church hymn was fine enough music for anybody." She adjusted the embroidery hoops on the napkin. "Alice just wanted to show off, that's the heart of the matter. Too much put on about her."

It was the inevitable reaction of the village to anything different. There was nothing the villagers resented more than a person who put on airs. The best tribute they could give a stranger was to say, "No put on about him. Just like one of us." They were satisfied with things as they were, and anybody who tried to prick that satisfaction annoyed them.

Nevertheless, new ideas and new diversions were

creeping into the village. When Alice Moeller took her phonograph upstairs to the playroom of the Red Men's Hall and taught a few of the more daring young the simple elements of the one-step to a record of *Poor Butterfly*, the parents were horrified, but the young were obviously delighted. The strongest impulse to change came from the teen-age boys and girls who were now going to high school in Altamont and Cobleskill, and there were learning to waltz and one-step, and later to fox trot. Gradually too, with the increase in automobiles, the village was becoming less isolated. More new visitors appeared. The outside world was moving in.

Life in the village, however, had changed little. Horses were still the ordinary power for transportation and for work. The grocery stores had just begun to offer bakery bread, brought by train each morning, but only a few households used it. There was still no electricity, no village water supply, and only the shadow of a sewage system. Perhaps five houses had acetylene lights, and the same houses had bathrooms with water toilets. The street lights had changed from kerosene lamps to gasoline lights pumped up and lit each night by old moustached Will Wands, who went around with a wax torch on a pole. But they were only lit on nights when the moon was not shining.

But if life in the village was changing only imperceptibly, the village itself suffered in this period its worst blow. The next hard-surfaced road to be constructed was the four-mile stretch from Esperance west to Sloansville. It started at the lower end of Main Street and went all the way through the village. To insure drainage at the sides, the road had to be raised. The long thin park in the middle of the street could no longer be retained nor the small triangle of park at the bridge entrance. The four big elms were ripped out and dumped into the crick, the piles of cannonballs were carted away, and concrete went down where the parks had been. The street began its advance toward the emptiness and barrenness that were to be characteristic of its new century. Before it had been a tree-bowered lane. Now it was on its way to being a barren passage-way.

None of the changes came easily to the older villagers. They resented having their lawns cut off. They resented the rumble automobiles were making when they passed over the loose planks of the bridge. They resented the new-fangled ideas. The young might protest the moral bans of the church. The church discipline might be reexamined. Dancing might now and then begin to replace the old kissing games. But the older people did not approve.

I well remember the first time I ever played a game on Sunday. A neighbor boy had come for a visit. It was after dinner. We sat on the sofa and started a game of two-handed pinochle with a deck of cards that he had brought with him. My mother, who was washing the dishes, must have sensed some-thing extraordinary going on, for she came to the parlor door with her hands dripping.

"What are you doing?" she said.

"Just playing a game of pinochle," I said.

I have said that my mother was never a strict disciplina-rian. She did not believe in forcing a child to do or not to do a thing unless there were pretty valid reasons for the forcing. And that day she stuck to her principle.

"Oh," she said and stood a moment in the doorway with her hands dripping, and then went back to the kitchen.

But to this day I can see the consternation in her eyes, the bewilderment, the frustration, the sense of something, perhaps she did not quite know what, violated. We put the cards away after a little while. The fun had gone out of the game.

The Transition Years

*I*n 1917 the United States entered Europe's war. I entered college and my father went back to farming. My father had a logical excuse now to do again what he most wanted to do. I no longer had to be near the Esperance depot. The nation needed farmers, needed food to send the boys to Europe, needed food to feed the workers in the ammunition factories. My mother was not happy about the move, but she had no logical objections to present. It would be unpatriotic not to do what was being asked. Mahala, who still lived with us, did not care one way or the other. She had never found any friends in the village. The Silvernail withdrawal was still strong in her. Nor had she found any particular happiness in our home. She and my mother had come to an unemotional tolerance of each other, roughened at moments into bickering. But we were all that was left in life for her. Place did not matter.

Perhaps it was a little comfort to her that we were going back to the Silvernail farm, not to Oak Nose, which was still in the hands of a tenant farmer. After the settlement of the Silvernail estate, my father, utilizing Mahala's share, had bought the Silvernail farm, paying for it partially from money saved from his work in the mill, mortgaging it for the rest.

Then, in the increasing demand for lumber caused by the rapid expansion of Schenectady and Albany, he had sold the timber from the woodlot of the Silvernail farm and with the proceeds paid off both mortgages. So for the first time in his life he was completely solvent. For the moment the future looked good to him.

Nancy Hanks, the spirited old mare, was dead, but my Uncle Barlow, long with an automobile and done forever now with horses, had given my father old Dan, a lanky good-tempered gelding, and my father bought a young horse, Brownie. That spring of 1917 I was given time off from high school to help on the farm. I remember it well, for the first job my father set me on was re-laying the stone walls around the cow pasture. I hated it. I could not get along working with my father. We were both self-willed. He was thorough and painstaking, I was swift and careless. We bickered in the fields as my mother and Mahala bickered in the house. But our bickerings never lasted the day out. "Never let the sun set on your bad feelings," was one of my father's mottoes. I remember the summer spent keeping cows out of clover and helping in the haying and harvest as one of the pleasant summers of my life.

In September I went to Cornell. There I floundered for two years, jumping from chemistry, into which a well-meaning high school teacher had turned me, to physics, and finally to my proper niche of English, but I never regretted my scientific beginning for it prevented me from slipping into the alien mysticism that has so clouded the literary thought of the mid-century. I had three scholarships, which partially paid my way, but I did such odd jobs as washing dishes, playing piano for a class of women doing reducing exercises to music, and doing secretarial work for the English department. But still my father had to turn over whatever he made on the farm to keep me going.

I began to write poetry. I came under the spell first of

Brownie and author, c. 1915, left, and Dan in old age, right.

Shelley and Keats, then of Emerson and Thoreau, and finally of Whitman and Sandburg, who was then at his peak.

I was also learning to dance well, to drink, to eat with finesse at table, and to be ashamed of my father's old-fashioned steel-rimmed spectacles and of my mother's work-worn hands. Like many country boys of that time, I was at first turned into a snob by college. Coming from farms and small villages, thrown together with children from rich families, eating at professors' houses with fine silver and old plate, next to women stylishly dressed and perfectly coiffed, we thought with dismay of the tawdry furniture of our homes, of the carelessly worn clothes of our parents.

Just how awful a snob I might have become I don't

The author at college graduation, 1921.

know had not a village woman, during one of my last summer vacations, set me back on my heels.

"That Freddie Lape," she said, "now he's going to college, his head's too big to swim with the likes of us."

I don't know what I had done to offend her. I never did know but, always a sensitive youth, I was deeply hurt when I heard her remark. For a while I hated her. But years later, when she was dead, I came to be grateful to her. For it was she who woke me up, who put my feet firm on the ground again. I began to take stock of myself and of the people about me and to form certain criteria of judgment and action that would apply to all persons in all places. It was the beginning of a real education for living.

It was during this same period that the village of Esperance adjusted itself to the new world, or was overwhelmed by it. Now the hard-surfaced roads were being extended, concrete or macadam, to Schoharie, to Cobleskill, to Schenectady. The first radio station of the area, WGY, began broadcasting from the General Electric Company in Schenectady, and each house had its little crystal set with a pair of earphones. Henry Ford having made the cheap automobile possible, more and more autos appeared in the village. The easy access to Schenectady took its first toll of the village businesses. When the owner of the drugstore died, no one thought the business worth taking over. The drugstores of Schenectady were too accessible. The building was bought by the Odd Fellow's Lodge, a lodge new to the village but already rivaling the Red Men's Lodge in importance. In these years the social life of the village was passing from the churches.

Inventions succeeded each other so rapidly in the first half of the century that some of them never had time to take root in a village like Esperance. In the large cities the street car came to sudden glory and to almost as sudden extinction. In Esperance the moving picture had such a career. By the early teens there was a nickelodeon in Cobleskill showing the *Perils of Pauline* or Theda Bara dying in the desert in *Bella Donna*, but it was not until about 1920 that Reefy Walker, a bachelor storekeeper who had for a few years kept a small store on the far side of the bridge, transformed an old barn behind the store into an auditorium, bought an old square piano, some wooden benches, and a moving picture projector. I was almost the only piano player in the vicinity, and summers when I was home from college I furnished the musical accompaniment to the silent movies. I well remember the pieces that were the stock in trade for the various thrillers and serials of the day, the little mysterious phrases that announced the villain, the music for storms and Indian raids, the battle music, the love music. But by this time the first radios were appearing, and automobile travel was becoming simpler. One could drive to Schenectady or Cobleskill and see the same pictures with better music and in more comfortable seats, or one could stay home and listen through a set of earphones to the distant voice of KDKA in Pittsburgh. So Reefy Walker's little movie theatre soon ceased to pay for itself and closed, and with that tiny gleam of success the movie industry brushed the little village once and never again.

Though the influx of new visitors to the village changed its life, more important in that change was the loss of young people who left the community. The daughters and sons of the hay dealer and of the insurance company president and of the merchants did not stay in the village. They went to Albany and New York and Philadelphia and Chicago. The sons of the farmers no longer stayed on the farm. They went to the cities, to the machine shops and the growing garages, for shorter hours, more money, the life of the cities. Farmers were buying automobiles now, the rural mail was carried by auto, not by horses. Nobody wanted any longer to live on the back dirt roads, so impassible to autos much of the year. Farms along the improved roads brought big prices, the backwoods farms next to nothing. Where formerly a farmer had planned to end his days on the farm, cared for by his children, now there were no children on the farm to keep him. They had all gone to the cities. A few of the farmers went there to live with their children, but most of them sold their farms and bought homes in the village in which to end their days. So common did this movement become that for a while the village almost became a home for the aged, particularly for old women, who seemed to outlive the men.

The life of the farmers too was changing. Though tractors were scarcely yet in use, automobiles and trucks furnished easy transport of fresh milk from the farms to the railroad, and local butter making began to disappear. The milk was shipped by railroad to large dairies in the cities. Now instead of raising all their own grain to feed their animals, farmers began to buy wheat and corn from Iowa and Nebraska and Illinois. The grist mills lost importance; their owners became bigger businessmen as middlemen. The self-sufficiency of the community was rapidly disappearing.

In the village the houses were transformed. First the barns were turned into garages and the driveways filled with stone so that cars would not get stuck in the mud. Then an electric line came to the village. Refrigerators replaced ice boxes, running water was easily possible. Cess pools were dug and flush toilets installed. When the surface wells proved inadequate, deep wells were drilled, forty to sixty feet sufficient then.

The installation of central heating systems changed the inside of the houses. Small rooms, built in the stove days to hold warmth in winter, now prevented free circulation of air for the pipeless furnaces so in favor because cheap. Partitions were knocked out, archways substituted for doors, pantries incorporated into kitchens. Parlors became living rooms. The kitchen range still remained, but a kerosene stove took its place for summer use.

A room that disappeared about this time was the little room that in the early days of the century was known as the den. This was the room of the man of the house. It was usually a room that had been a small bedroom off the parlor but later converted into a place where the man could have his papers, his desk, his smoking equipment, his own little retreat. Now with central heating the partition between this room and the parlor was removed and the two rooms incorporated into one. The woman of the house moved her sewing machine into the opened nook, and the man was shoved out into the new garage or later into a room in the cellar.

As the man lost his den, he also lost his spittoon. For years the spittoon had been part of the furnishing of any parlor or sitting room. The early years of the century had been years of pipe smoking, cigar smoking, and chewing of tobacco, and to do any of these without occasional spitting was, to the man of the time, unthinkable. I remember a remark of one of the village men at the time when a fireplace in a house was coming to be a status symbol. "A fireplace," he said, "is such a noble place to spit." But cigarette smoking was on the increase. Chewing tobacco and spitting were becoming unpopular. Women were ashamed to have spittoons in their rooms. The spittoons disappeared.

Another feature of status, sun porches, spread over the village. These were not new additions to the houses. They were the same old Victorian stoops. Soon almost every homeowner was having frames of glass fitted in the spaces between the pillars. It did not matter that half of these sun porches faced the north or were so shaded by trees that they never received the sun. It was fashionable to have a sun porch. One or two houses, it is true, did have new porches built either on the side or the back of the house, screened in summer and glassed in winter, but the idea of a porch only for the intimate use of the family was still foreign to the village. A sun porch was a place for neighborly gossip and for watching the movement on the street.

Along with the changes to the houses themselves were the changes of the activities inside the house. The automobile was bringing the cities and their markets within easy reach of the village, and manufactured products were replacing homemade products. Home vegetable gardens were beginning to wane. The home preservation and storage of meats was decreasing. There was no longer even a butcher in the village. Meat was peddled from house to house on a delivery truck from a butcher in Schoharie. The village dressmaker now found little to do. Women bought ready-made dresses in the cities or from the mail order catalogs. Embroidering was going out of fashion. Bakery bread was replacing home-baked bread, though the baking of pies and cakes still held its own. Bathing in a tub before the kitchen stove had moved to bathing in the bathtub in the new bathroom. With safety razors, shaving entered the home. And childbearing and death were beginning to move out of the houses.

Entertainment too was moving out of the house and away from the churches. Sunday was no longer the headache day of my childhood. Since Sunday was the one day a man of business was free to enjoy his automobile, he took advantage of it and went on a trip instead of going to church. And if a ride in an auto was all right on Sunday, why not a game of cards? And if a game of cards, why not a little dancing, at home of course, to the music of the new Victrola? Or even, for the daring, an evening to the movies in Schenectady, where after a bitter struggle between the church forces and the mercantile forces, moving picture theatres were permitted to be open on Sundays.

Dancing was becoming socially popular, not square dancing but ballroom dancing, the fox trot and all its variations. The country fiddler and anything like the old bean bakes of the Chapman House were almost extinct. Dancing was done at parties either to the music of a phonograph or to the music of a single piano played by anybody who could be inveigled into playing *Margie* or *I Ain't Got Nobody* while the rest danced. The old kissing games were dying rapidly. None of the social groups of the village had as yet dared to hold a dance with a hired orchestra, but at each party dancing became more popular.

I remember vividly one such party. It must have been about 1920. I had learned to play all the new dance tunes in my fraternity house at Cornell, and in Esperance I was always being asked to play the piano while somebody danced. There was also in the village Jen VanVechten, the wife of the insurance company president. She was in her sixties then, probably the most wealthy woman in the village, full of joy of life and of music, and by the privilege of wealth oblivious to the moral inhibitions of the village. She had learned only a year or two earlier to play the saxophone. Any drums fascinated her. Drums were becoming increasingly important for the steady rhythm of the fox trot, and she had induced the owner of the village band's bass drum to bring it to the party. She herself brought her saxophone, two tambourines, and a bazooka. Seating herself on the dais of the meeting room at the Red Men's Hall, next to me at the piano, she amused herself all evening banging the bass drum to my music, grabbing her saxophone and playing it until she ran out of breath, dropping the saxophone and smacking out a few measures with the tambourines, and jabbing the bazooka into her mouth and rasping out a chorus or two. Rhythm was natural to her in every movement of her body.

"Oh, if I were thirty years younger, I'd start a dance orchestra," she said.

She was born just that thirty years too early. Had she been young she might have become, at the height of the jazz period, one of the great names in the country. But by that time she was dead.

The party of that night remains vivid in my mind not only because of Jen VanVechten, but because it was a symbol of the new era of freedom for the individual, of a breaking away from the old rigid prohibitions and empty moral restrictions, an opening of personality that was to flourish, all too shortly, until the succession of wars and patriotic fervor closed it again in the middle of the century.

But it did not affect the old guard. Abbie McCarty never learned to play a saxophone, or even to have a Victrola. She stuck to her parlor organ.

In 1922 I began a brief career as an instructor in English at Cornell. My salary was $1,200 a year. Out of the prospects I bought my first automobile, one of the cutdown Fords so popular then among college boys. It had wire wheels fastened to the axles only by large brass hubcaps which were constantly unscrewing and letting the wheels drop off. Once on one of the curving hills of Ithaca one of the back wheels came off, rolled ahead of the car, and zipped neatly between two women walking down the sidewalk, fortunately harming nothing except their nerves. The car had no self-starter. It had a windshield wiper that one worked by hand and an emergency brake that never worked, so that if I stalled on a hill, I was in a desperate situation. I did so once in the middle of traffic on Broadway hill in Schenectady, in front of a trolley car. Fortunately my cousin Claramae was along and stretched her foot to the foot brake while I got out and cranked. The fuel system worked by gravity, and without a tank of gas at least half full I could not get up a steep hill except by turning around and backing up.

The first time I drove it home I got stuck in a mudhole

within sight of the house. My father without remark harnessed Dan and Brownie and pulled me out.

That year Mahala died, of no sickness, only a wearing out of all the body. In the end my mother had to help her eat, and she said, "You fed Jane in her last days too, didn't you?"

During my second year of teaching I was called home by a telegram. My father was sick with an acute kidney infection. He was delirious when I arrived. For a week we despaired of his life. Every day, early in the morning, Dr. Paul Moore came driving up the dirt road in his horse and gig. He was already in his sixties, but he took the daily drive and call as a matter of course and charged, if I remember correctly, seventy-five cents a day for his visits. And he saved my father's life.

At the same time he treated me. The too strenuous social life at Cornell, with the too much drinking of bootleg liquor, had thrown me into a nervous indigestion and a mawkish melancholy state of mind. "Exercise," Dr. Paul Moore said. "Walk ten miles a day." And then he turned me on Young's *Night Thoughts*.

But for my father there was no such easy solution. His illness had sapped his strength. Probably he could have recovered in time and with temporary hired help kept the farm going. Had the decision been his alone, I'm sure he would have tried. But my mother had had her fill of farming. I had accepted a job teaching the next fall at Stanford, in California, and my mother could not accept the responsibility of the farm and its lonely life. So she convinced my father to give up farming, go back to the village, and resume the watch-repairer's trade. He could not be induced yet to sell the farm, but all the farm machinery and all the stock except the horse Brownie were put up for auction. My father was his own auctioneer. It was a rainy day, the crowd was small, the things went for small prices, and my father stood there in the rain auctioning them off, the rain

Herman Lape as auctioneer, 1915.

dripping from the brim of his felt hat, and all the dreams of the future dripping away like the rain.

He and my mother moved back to the same house in which we had lived during my high school years. It was an old brown two-story house with a cupola, sitting back from the street, with a low square-pillared porch across the front and one side, and a **Y** sidewalk leading in from the street between lawns and flowerbeds. Its former owner, the village painter, was now dead, but his widow still lived in half of the house. The rooms were large, the front ones with French doors, and its porch was a pleasant place, back from the noise of the streets, where automobiles were continually passing, for the Cherry Valley Turnpike had become highway U.S. 20, one of the main east-west arteries of the state.

It had no conveniences. My gift, perhaps to salve my conscience from running away from the responsibility of home,

Herman Lape as a watch repairer, c. 1900.

was to have electricity installed in our half of the house, but there was still no running water and therefore no bathroom. There was one other liability. The house, sitting back, was just in line with a neighbor's barn, and the neighbor's pigpen was just across from one of the kitchen windows.

My father brought out his watch repairing tools that had been so long stored. He set up his work bench in a corner of the kitchen, close to the cookstove. On the huge silver maple on the street he hung his old sign, a hand-carved wooden watch with the hands balanced at twenty past eight, said by some to commemorate the hour Lincoln was shot, and his name across the front. It was to hang there the rest of his life.

My mother, always restless, now went to work to earn herself some spending money. The latest occupation for women of the village was sewing covers on baseballs. The old shop in the village where the women formerly stitched underwear had been turned into a shop for covering baseballs, but many of the women, like my mother, preferred to work at home. A clamp was installed in front of another kitchen window, and there my mother worked. The balls came in bags, all wound and ready for the covers. A ball was put in the clamp, two covers fitted on it, pulled together wth pliers, and then stitched tight. My mother worked long hours and made little money, but she was happy to be in the village again where her friends could drop in and gossip with her while she worked.

Fred Brown was also sewing balls for a living. He used to come often in the evenings and visit with my father. Tiny, the energetic and strange aunt, had died, but the thin old withered mother still lived, and Fred took care of her in his slovenly way, helped out by occasional gifts of baked dishes from the neighbors.

As Fred grew older his passion for watches increased. He had a collection of them, and he was always bringing them to my father to be regulated. Approximate regulations never satisfied him, he wanted perfection. If a watch gained a minute a week, he would bring it back for further regulating.

He had by now become the town weather prophet. He always predicted ahead of time the severity of winters and the probable rainfall or snowfall for the ensuing months. Unfortunately, his day by day storm predictions were often inaccurate, so much so that the villagers often went on the assumption that the weather would probably be the opposite of what Fred said it would be. In all spells of violent cold, his thermometer reports were the ones that went in to the newspapers, for his house stood in a spot that seemed to be the focus of cold in the valley's curve.

In these later days his typewriter came into more use. He wrote the personals of the village, first for the county newspapers, from which he received no pay except a subscription, and later for the city papers, from which he made a pittance. Actually I think he did it because it gave him something to type. In those years he often needed something to fill his hours.

He became a village figure. He never missed the morning and evening deliveries of mail at the post office. As if his feet were too big for the village sidewalks, he always walked in the middle of the street. Even after the village's main street had become the thoroughfare of U.S. 20, he would still plod up and down it, in sunshine, rain, or snow, while the cars and trucks whizzed past and around him. The villagers always said he would be killed some day, but he never was.

Bus service was good then on U.S. 20, and Fred, lonely, got in the habit of walking the eighth of a mile from his home to the highway to wave and shout hello to the bus drivers going past. Finally the drivers grew into the habit of stopping a moment. They would ask him about the weather. They thought him a better prophet than the villagers thought him and came to depend upon his word for probable road conditions the next day.

By the time I left for California my father was beginning to adapt himself to village life. Radio programs were now beginning to be a regular feature of daily living. WGY, a pioneer in broadcasting, was also for the moment a pioneer in presenting good programs. It had its own small chamber orchestra and its quartet of singers, and it broadcast lectures as well. This too was the day when the National Broadcasting Company was presenting a varied assortment of programs, soap operas in the afternoons, Amos n' Andy at supper time, and often good plays or concerts at night. Both my father and my mother listened to these programs. My father too, like Fred Brown, had discovered the pleasure of the morning gossip period at the post office while the mail was being sorted and the gossip fests at the grocery stores. He now had more time to read. In his later years he had turned to philosophy (Spinoza was his favorite), and he was constantly on the outlook for new books which he would buy or which I, when I was home, could bring him from the Schenectady library.

So while I set out to widen my mind with mountains, the Canadian Rockies, Yosemite, the Pacific, and to plague my body with the hard drinking of the twenties, my father, remaining in Esperance, set his mind on as wide a voyage into the unknowns of existence.

The End of an Era

*I*n 1930 in the days just before the Depression spread beyond the financial centers of the country, I came back East to live, I thought, the affluent life of a writer. I had taught at Stanford for five years, but I had come home every year for the summer vacation, so that my link with the village always remained close. I had become increasingly dissatisfied with graduate study, which was then obviously becoming necessary for success in a teaching career. I had sold a story to the then flourishing *Collier's* for three hundred dollars and had bought a second-hand Nash touring car, in which I drove back East. I still had a little of my last year's salary left, and I was cocksure of success.

In the meantime, just to have some quick spending money, I began to play in a dance orchestra. Our outfit consisted of the Brand brothers—John who played the drums and Perley who played both saxophone and violin—and myself at the piano. Our jobs at first were in open-air dance pavilions, one in Duanesburg, and another new and more successful one between Esperance and Sloansville, called the Rustic. Liquor was sold at neither, but by this time the college stag lines had reached Esperance, and dancing was the rage. Another strange phenomenon was appearing. That almost extinct animal, the square dance of the Chapman House bean bakes, was raising its head. Perley had learned to fiddle as a child and knew all the old square dance tunes.

Our repertoire was invariably a fox trot, a waltz, and a square dance. It soon became obvious that the square dances were the most popular numbers. They were attracting not only a few of the old timers but an increasing number of couples from the cities, persons who had never square danced before in their lives but who found the rhythms and the intricacies of the dances exciting. As the popularity of the dances increased, we added a banjo player and a second saxophone. We were much in demand, for the very reason that we could play both rounds and squares. Our jazz numbers were not exactly Paul Whiteman, but they were sufficient to their crowd. In our square dances we were lighting the dawn of a new era in dancing in the United States, and more distantly, a new era of popular music, the pseudo-folk ballad.

My father, I could see over the years, was gradually accepting his new life. Not that he was ever really happy in his work. The watches were becoming smaller and smaller, the tiny screws and wheels more and more difficult for his fingers to hold, fingers that had enlarged and roughened with farm work. He was always losing some tiny part in the dirt on the floor at his feet, and then would begin a hunting, a sweeping of the floor, and a miniscule examination of all the swept-up dirt, while my father grew more and more unnerved and complained bitterly, "Oh, how I hate it, how I hate it!" and sometimes sobbed. Those were the days that I could not face him, or my mother, or even myself. How much was I responsible for this misery?

But these were really the unusual days. Most of the time he was content. He had a vegetable garden, which was always without a weed. He enjoyed the mailtime gossiping at the post office. He enjoyed talking with the literary friends I was making outside of the village. He enjoyed sitting on the porch in the

Herman Lape, c. 1936.

evenings, smoking his pipe and watching the chimney swifts swooping over the tops of the trees along the street, his mind abroad on its own adventure.

The village, however, was approaching its lowest ebb. It had been too far from either Schenectady or Albany to have shared in the suburban expansion of the first World War. Instead, it had lost its industries, its stores, its self-sufficiency.

Now it was losing its trees. The Dutch elm disease had not yet threatened, but the old ladies who now made up half of the inhabitants of the village were always getting afraid that one of the huge elms which overshadowed their houses would drop limbs on the roofs. They had no money to hire tree surgeons to treat the elms and wire the limbs, and since they made up a good share of the taxpayers of the village, neither did the village have money to spend on tree repair. So when one of the old elms showed a dead limb, down came the tree. The worst of it was that scarcely anybody bothered to plant a young tree in place of the removed elm. Gradually Main Street was becoming as bare as the street of a mining town.

A new invention now added its sores to the already peeling skin. This was an artificial paper asphalt house siding that could be applied cheaply in strips, simulating either brick or wood siding. Since this extra coat of siding was a fine insulation and made winter heating cheaper, a good third of the houses of the village had their basically well-proportioned wood siding covered by this yellow brown or dull red scum, its lines usually slightly awry, so that certain sections of the village came to have the look of a shanty town.

But the real loss of identity came to Esperance with the removal of the old covered bridge. Even though Theodore Burr had not considered the automobile when he built his bridge, it had for twenty years been carrying all the traffic of U.S. 20, now a main cross-continent route. All day long the bridge shook and shivered with passing autos and trucks. The two-inch planks that made its flooring were always loose. They roared all day like a continuous thunderstorm.

For the second time engineers condemned the bridge. They put a weight limit on trucks passing over it. They put up warnings that anybody passing over it did so at his own risk. The traffic did not decrease. The bridge went on shivering and resounding with its thunder.

One spring frost got in one of the piers, and a quarter of it—an upstream quarter—tumbled into the water. Since there was no new bridge forthcoming, a contractor was hired to splice a new concrete quarter on the cracked pier. "Maybe it'll stay a few years," he said. It stayed.

Then the state ground slowly to action. Money was appropriated for a new bridge. Surveyors came. Engineers came. A contractor came. Steam shovels and cement mixers roared and sputtered a few feet downstream. Traffic still rumbled over the old bridge, but the new one grew. It was not a thing of beauty. It was of steel, efficient, nondescript.

When the new bridge was opened there was a celebration. There were two bands, speeches, fireworks, crowds. The mayor of Albany made a speech at the cutting of the ribbon. There was dancing at night on the concrete floor of the new bridge. I headed a committee to sell souvenirs of the old bridge. We had pieces of an old bridge timber sawed into little plaques and stamped with the date. The good-looking girls of the village sold them. What the money went to I can't remember.

Amie Clayton, old Amie Clayton now, was at the celebration. In that day of the automobile, he still traveled the roads only by foot. It was a common sight to pass him at night trudging along the side of the highway, his shoulders bent, his satchel swinging from his arm, an old coat slapping around his thighs. Sometimes he slept in the upstairs room of the firehouse in the village or in the haymow of a barn, or if he was near Burtonsville, then in the little house on the island in the middle of the crick, where he still lived with his mother, the only friend of his whole later life. He was too old to jig to the accordion any longer. He carried with him now only his satchel of patent medicines and pins.

But Fred Brown had not been on hand to predict the weather for the day of the bridge opening. His mother had died not long after Tiny. Nobody was ever left more completely alone. All his life, except for the few years he lived with us at Oak Nose, his intimates had been two old women. Nature had made him, like Amie, ill-shaped and unprepossessing. He never had an intimate friend.

He was no good at keeping house by himself. He cooked food poorly or not at all. The dirt accumulated, and he left it. The house was small, but it must have seemed tremendous to him in those last days.

The neighbors often brought him food and sometimes came in and cleaned the house for him. But in spite of this, he could not take care of himself. Badly cooked food further ruined his digestion. He was always having severe colds. One day a neighbor going to the door found it locked and heard Fred inside groaning. He was rolling on the floor in pain. He did not know what was the matter with him. The matter was a burst appendix. Dr. Paul Moore got somebody to take him to Schenectady to the hospital. It was in the days before antibiotics. He died there two days later, alone.

When the lights of the bridge celebration were put out, the old bridge stood a few feet upstream, dark and silent. It was 117 years old, a unique relic of its era. It should have been saved as a monument. A few of us in the village tried to save it. But most of the villagers were against us. They thought it an eyesore. They had heard the rumble of traffic over its planks too many years. They talked of fire hazard, cost of upkeep, danger to curiousity seekers. Mere excuses. They didn't want relics. When a thing was dead, it ought to be dead, buried, out of mind. So the old bridge had to go. The state gave the contract for tearing it down to the same contractor who had built the new bridge.

The dismantling started the next day. The contractor tore off the roof, the side shingles, the plate boards. The naked frame of pine timber stretched across the crick, a skeleton rising from bulks of stone and concrete piers. The pine of the timbers was for the most part as solid as the day it was put in, aged and brown on the surface, but within white and strong.

They started to rip out the pins and pull the framework apart piece by piece. That was too much work. The timbers stuck. In disgust the contractor decided to burn down the framework. He set fire to one end of the first arch. The timbers burned, the end of the arch burned loose from its abutment, the crowds gathered to watch the span fall.

It didn't fall. One hundred and seventeen years old, the naked skeleton of a span arched across space and held itself rigid by its one clasp on the solid pier at the end.

They burned the solid end, and the span went down. The two other spans were taken down by the same siege. After the timbers had been cleaned away, they broke down the old piers, the walls of masonry, the concrete splice. Down deep, the foundations of stone and interlocked hemlock timbers, the ancient foot of the bridge, remained. Those hemlock timbers, water soaked for over a hundred years, were still strong, stronger than anything that was being built in Esperance at that moment.

Had the bridge been saved, it could have preserved the historical identity of Esperance, a rare landmark. But the residents of Esperance then were not interested in preserving anything. They were interested in progress, whatever that meant to them, the glamor of the new plus more money in the pocket.

So the village and I reached the depth of our adversity at about the same time. By the mid-thirties the Depression had extended its fingers to all of the small villages of the nation, and in the industrial centers luxury products like literature were indispensable. Magazines were folding monthly. No longer was a promising young novelist greeted with a smile by publishing houses.

I was lucky then that our dance orchestra was still in demand, though we had come down to playing for three dollars a man a night. But we no longer played in dance halls like the Rustic. Prohibition had gone, and beer parlors had come in. The drunkenness of the college campuses of the twenties (I once saw six boys dragged out by their feet during one downtown dance in Ithaca) was now spreading over the nation. Prohibition had completely transformed the social attitude toward drinking in Esperance. The saloon of the Chapman House had been considered the disgrace of the village, but on Saturday nights the beer parlor that went up where the Rustic had been called forth the young of the countryside. Henceforth these beer parlors were to be the places where we played, along the highways, on the outskirts of Schenectady, over in the smaller Mohawk Valley towns. They were ugly places. There was usually a fight or two during the evening, nothing very serious, some maudlin shouting and pushing, and maybe a torn shirt or two. But the popularity of the dances continued, and by them for a few years I made my living.

I used to look at myself objectively sometimes. With a cigarette dangling from my lower lip, holding my head back to keep the smoke out of my eyes, the air about me foul with the smell of beer, pounding out *Turkey in the Straw* on a broken-down old square piano with half of the ivories missing and part of the bass keys not working, I used to laugh ironically at the ditch that life had thrown me into. Where were Keats and Emerson and Whitman now? Well, they were dead, and I at least was alive.

I had gone back to Oak Nose to live. The last succession of tenant farmers had left it a shambles, the land untended, the roof of the barn a sieve, the house dirty and splashed inside with blue and green and strawberry paint over peeling wallpaper. In my zeal for reconstruction I nearly tore the house apart, stripped off the wallpaper, stripped lath and plaster from the kitchen ceiling to expose the beams, knocked out partitions until a stairway nearly floated in space and the house was so open inside that it was almost impossible to heat in winter because all the warm air rushed upstairs. Fortunately, I could not destroy the proportions of the building.

I bought antiques for furniture, cheap then, attractive, but the chairs always collapsing. I made a large vegetable garden, from which I got half my food. I reroofed the barn, tore down the wagonhouse and with the lumber transformed one of the haymows of the main barn into a studio. I began to reforest the lean hillsides with pine and spruce and fir seedlings which the state forestry service was offering cheaply. The rich flats were going back to weeds and brush.

In the strawberry season I brought my mother up to pick wild strawberries. This was the one feature of farm living that had been a joy to her, and in her old age it was a delight to find a good strawberry patch in a field and sit down in the middle of it with her pail and pick while the field sparrows sputtered near their nests.

My father looked upon all my antics with tolerant amusement. He was pleased, I think, that somebody was doing something with Oak Nose, even if that something was a long way from what he conceived the purpose of land to be. But I could rarely bring him up to the farm. Evidently he still did not like to face the scenes of his disappointment.

It was a comfort to me that in those years he and I had come to understand each other. I still had the old Nash car, and Sundays we used to go for trips, or sometimes in the summer we went for a week to Maine or Massachusetts, to the ocean. He had in the last years grown interested in geology, and wherever we went he collected rocks. He carried a hammer and a basket on the seat beside him, and whenever we would go through a new road cut he would say enthusiastically, "Stop!" and I would stop and he would get out and look in the fresh cut for crystal inclusions or types of rock not yet in his collection.

In the village the elms continued to go down. The old storekeepers died, and the stores grew smaller. One grist mill remained, but it was only a feed store, it ground no grain. Not half of the farms were cultivated. They went back to weeds. The men who lived in the farmhouses commuted to Schenectady to work. The local grocers had a hard time because in the cities the supermarkets were beginning, and with their bigger volume of trade were able to offer cheaper prices than the local grocers.

Much of the back country was going to wilderness. A far-seeing governor, Al Smith, had instituted a program of reforestation. All the high plateaus away from the main roads, now deserted farms, were planted with pine and spruce and larch, to be forest where once oats and corn and buckwheat had grown.

I can describe the villagers of that day only as apathetic. They were interested in little that lay outside their daily lives. They were interested neither in what Esperance had been nor in what it might be for the future. It was about this time that Storrs Seeley gave his library to the village. The Seeley family had been former residents, remnants of the intellectual group of Esperance of the past century, but like the family of Dr. Paul Moore, the Seeley family too was running out. The two sisters and the brother had no children. They still loved the village and had never sold their old house on Main Street. It was closed all winter, but in the summer the girls, now in their sixties, would spend their vacations there. The house contained a couple of genuine Chippendale chairs and some other rare pieces of furniture.

But the Seeleys were all getting old. They were soon going to close up their home in New York and go live with a niece in Amsterdam. So Storrs decided to give his library to the village of Esperance. It was a small library but an excellent one, from classics to modern fiction. Esperance, unfortunately, was not yet ready for a library. There was not even a place to put the books. Since the Seeleys had been Presbyterians, the Ladies Aid of the Presbyterian church agreed to take care of the books. They made a place for them in the upper story of the Presbyterian manse, a fine old home which had been so distorted in remodeling that one had to go upstairs by a rickety stairway through a trap door, which one pushed up over his head as he ascended.

There the ladies put the books, and there they let them lie. I read most of the nonfiction, and my mother, who in her later years had become an avid reader of novels with happy endings, went through all the volumes of fiction, from Walter Scott to Mary Roberts Rinehart. But I think we were almost the only ones who ever made use of Storrs' gift. The books gathered dust in their inaccessible quarters, and when the Presbyterian Church came on bad times and the manse was sold, the books were lost.

The Schoharie itself was going into disuse. The villagers working in the cities and commuting had less time to fish or swim, and their children seemed to care less about it. New York City had built a dam on the upper reaches of the Schoharie at Gilboa for a water supply, and this curtained considerably the amount of water in the crick at Esperance during the summer. The remnants of the old dam in Esperance had long washed away. There was less quiet water to make good skating in winter, but nobody seemed to want to skate in winter anyway. Refrigerators had superseded the need for ice, so ice was no longer cut. Housewives could buy fresh fish in the city markets and not be bothered by the cleaning of them. The state conservation department had seen fit to stock the crick with walleye pike, a larger fish than the small mouth black bass but not a good game fish. The old fishermen were dying off, and their sons did not carry on the enthusiasm. Fishing was becoming more and more the sport of outsiders who came from the cities in cars, fished the day, and went home. Most of the villagers began to ignore fishing.

Swimming was still popular, particularly at the old swimming hole, but it was no longer limited to the village boys. Now outsiders coming with cars began to frequent the swimming hole. They brought bathing suits, to which the village boys still remained scornful. But it was the time of growing women's rights too, and the girls were demanding their share of the fun. Why should the boys be allowed to swim nude? Girls dared not go near the place. The controversy raged, but it had not yet come to a settlement. Nude bathing by boys at the swimming hole persisted until about the mid-thirties. By that time the first summer cottage had gone up along the crick close to the swimming hole, dumping its sewage into the crick. It was the beginning of the complete pollution of the Schoharie.

Annie Denison no longer lived in the little house on the way to the swimming hole. In her later years, after her mother died, she was put in an institution, where it was said she was happy. Probably she would have been happier had she lived in an institution from childhood on, among others equally peculiar, so that being peculiar carried no stigma.

But the villages still had some amusement for their spare moments. In the afternoons they could always watch the squabble between Mrs. Heaton and Clara Krepline. These two had become curiosities only by becoming neighbors. Clara Krepline had run a boarding house in the village for years. Her husband had worked in the grist mills as a helper most of his life, but like many of the village men, he was neither a steady worker nor a good money earner. Clara's boarders were sometimes summer visitors from New York, sometimes hunters in the fall, and in times of road construction, the road workers. But when overnight visitors became frequent with the increase of automobile traffic, Clara put out a TOURISTS sign, and for a year or two did a flourishing business.

But about this time Mrs. Heaton, an outsider, bought the old home of Doctor Norwood, next to Clara's house. Mrs. Heaton came from the city and had modern ideas about a home. She, like I, knocked out partitions. She put in hardwood floors and a bathroom (Clara's house still had only a privy), she had the house repainted inside and out and a new garage built in the back. Then she put out a TOURISTS sign not ten feet away from Clara's sign. Clara was furious. The nerve of the woman, an outsider, to come in and compete with an established business!

From then on the two women hated each other like two setting hens. And there was something of the setting hen in the actions of each. Mrs. Heaton was erect and slow moving, white haired, with fair complexion, with ample bosom, the hen who walks slowly about her chicks and then without warning gives a peck at an intruder. Clara was plump and round faced, black haired and nervous, the restless, fussy, always-clucking hen.

They would sit on their porches in the late afternoons, when tourists were apt to be stopping for a night's lodging, and if a car stopped anywhere near either house, both would jump up and advance from their porches, Mrs. Heaton in her magnificent stately way, Clara with her impatient angry fluttering, out to the sidewalk and upon the unwary tourist. Whoever got the prey led it triumphantly into her house, while the other glared helplessly from her empty porch. Women used to come and sit on nearby porches late in the afternoon and gossip and watch the fun.

Their enmity never ceased, even when the reason for their feud was gone. Soon cabins began to be built everywhere along the highways. The cabins caught the tourist trade. Nobody stopped any longer in front of Clara's house or in front of

Mrs. Heaton's house. But the two women hated each other as long as they lived.

Another diversion was to see which one of her hats, or what kind of a crazy new one, Abbie McCarty would be wearing. Abbie was still one of the telephone operators. Her father had long been dead, but her mother, nearly a hundred years old, was still alive, and nobody ever received more loving care than Mrs. McCarty got from Abbie. She had become an invalid in her last years, and Abbie cared for her completely without help, fixing meals that her mother could eat during her absence at the telephone office and rushing home the moment her work was over. The passing of her figure, with erect bearing and determined stride, up and down the street to the office and back home again, was as regular an event as the arrival of the buses or the mails. But what gave Abbie's arrivals variety were her hats.

Abbie's hats were as distinctive as those of the Queen Mother Mary. As a matter of fact they were quite similar, but Abbie wore hers at a more jaunty angle. There was no longer any milliner in Esperance, so Abbie had to buy her hats from the mail order houses, where she also bought her clothes. Both were outlandish. Having been brought up in the Victorian era, she still considered ankles were to support the body and not to be seen. In the twenties she had never yielded to short skirts but continued to wear long swishing skirts when flappers were going around with rolled stockings and skirts to their knees.

The change in morals and habits shocked her. She never grew reconciled to dancing and card playing and jazz music. Hymns were her music, and she sometimes played them on the organ still in her parlor. The interior of her house was a curiosity shop. On the walls of the parlor were the usual large framed pictures of her parents, other photographs of her relatives, sacred pictures, match holders. All the stands were loaded with pictures, cards, curios, baskets, little toys of glass, plastic figures, knicknacks which pleased her fancy and which she either ordered from the mail order houses or bought at the ten cent store when somebody took her to the city.

She still kept her interest in flowers and always carried a bouquet from her garden to church each Sunday during the summer, or made a special bouquet for the funerals of old villagers. But she had less time now for her annual gardens and began to plant things that took less care. Now she set in her yard the new shrubs and trees that nurseries were offering — Japanese quince, beautybush, variegated juniper. She even planted a blue spruce between her parlor and the street, which soon began to overshadow the house.

Her mother died at last. When Abbie was sixty-five she was forced to retire from the telephone office, much to her chagrin. She never thoroughly took to retirement. With the death of her mother, her main purpose in living was gone. She now transferred her strong ties of affection to a grand-nephew, whose schooling she watched with pride and to which she contributed money. But she could never bridge the gap between her generation and the new, and though she wanted desperately to help her nephew and her grand-nephew, she was to them as much a problem as an assistance. How did one face with equanimity bringing to a graduation exercise Aunt Abbie with her outlandish clothes and her even more outlandish hats? The failure of each to understand the other was one of the comedy-tragedies of the period, when moral standards and habits of living were changing so rapidly.

Though Abbie's life had never been dramatic, her death had its element of drama. She died when the village was suffering from the worst flood of the century. The crick was a roaring torrent. It had flooded all the lower sections of the village. The new Esperance bridge was closed to traffic. The dam at Gilboa, built to hold the water of the Schoharie for New

York City, was in danger of breaking. Residents of the village moved for the night to stay with relatives and friends in the hills, safe against disaster.

No one then had time to worry about the dead. So Abbie's funeral, which she had wanted to be at the altar of the Methodist church to which she had dedicated so many hours of her life, had to be delayed until the waters went down. And even then the routine of village life was so badly unsettled that the funeral was held only in the basement Sunday school room. No flowers from her own garden or from neighbor's gardens honored her body, only the impersonal wreaths of the undertaking trade.

She was the last of the old local curiosities to die. And with her death, the era of intense individuality disappeared from the village and left way for the uniformity of dress, habits, and thought that were to be characteristic of the middle of the century.

Now the century nears its end. The transformation of the village of Esperance is complete. The church sheds are gone, as are the covered wooden bridge, the elms along Main Street, the two grist mills, the livery stable, the sewing shops, the shoe repairing shop, the drug store, two of the grocery stores, the ice cream parlor, and, last, the telephone office. The only garage is a mile out of the village. The Red Men's Lodge has ceased to exist, and the old Red Men's hall, that recreation center, is an auction house for antiques. The old village is dead.

But a new Esperance now begins to look both to the future and to the past. It has a new brick post office. The old insurance company is housed in a modern brick building. The barn that held the proudly stepping horses of the insurance company president has been transformed into a well-equipped firehouse, with first aid ambulance service. There is no barber, but there are two hairdressers. And there is a museum in the old wooden schoolhouse.

In the museum relics are the household and farm implements of my youth. There are the cradles that were used to cut oats. There is the cream separator that used to run in the milk room at Oak Nose. There is the Victor talking machine that used to play the *American Patrol March*. There is an old 1900 washing machine and the copper tank that used to be set on the back of the kitchen stove on washdays to heat water for the washing. There is some of the ironstone china on which we used to eat our meals. And there is the Silvernail quilt made by Rachel Silvernail in 1863, with the date and the Civil War flag and Rachel's initials on the corners.

But it takes more than artifacts to capture the feeling of an era. How can a museum recreate the sardonic "Aw-w-w-w-w," of Fred Brown, or the tinny wheeze of Amie Clayton's cheap accordion while he jigged for pennies, or the rattle of the loose planks of the old bridge under the horse and lumber wagon or under the early automobiles? And how can it bring back the scent of perennial phlox on a warm summer afternoon?

Sometimes now when I walk past a garden in July and catch that sweet odor of perennial phlox, the era comes back to me. For the moment I am sitting on the stoop in the village, and on the stoop of the house next door two women sit embroidering and gossiping, from down the street comes the sound of Dietta Ball's player piano rippling out the *International Bag*, and Abbie McCarty comes walking fast up the flagstone sidewalk, hurrying to her little house to get a late dinner for her mother.

A FARM AND VILLAGE BOYHOOD

was composed in eleven-point VIP Goudy Old Style and leaded two points
with display type also in Goudy Old Style
by Utica Typesetting Company, Inc.;
printed on 55-pound Warren acid-free Antique Cream paper,
Smyth-sewn and bound over boards in Columbia Bayside Chambray
by Maple-Vail Book Manufacturing Group, Inc.;
and published by

SYRACUSE UNIVERSITY PRESS

SYRACUSE, NEW YORK